HARLEY~
DAVIDSON

The Living Legend

HARLEY~DAVIDSON

The Living Legend

William Green

CRESCENT BOOKS
New York

This 1992 edition published by CRESCENT BOOKS distributed by Outlet Book Company, Inc., a Random House Company 225 Park Avenue South, New York, New York 10003.

Printed and bound in Italy.

ISBN 0-517-06683-1

Photographs supplied by Andrew Gray and William Green.

Page 1 *Relaxing in the sun at Seabreeze Street, Ormond Beach, on a Super Glide.*
The oil spill is not from the Custom XLCH Harley.
Pages 2-3 *Top left: The Harley-Davidson logo.*
Centre left: A show-winner Harley Sportster.
Bottom left: Sliding, three-speed transmission lever on the gasoline tank of an 11F.
Centre: 1962 Sportster with 80 cu inch engine.
Right: The Barbarian – paint by Kent Imperial.
This page: 1970 Sportster street racer style.

CONTENTS

The First Years

Willie G. and his son Bill Davidson, both long-standing Harley employees. Willie G. is the Head of Design and the man who has shaped the image of Harley-Davidson today.

The turn of the century in the United States brought with it innovation, new-found prosperity, remarkable and important discoveries and hitherto unknown excitement. The horse, for thousands of years man's faithful partner in travel and adventure, was on the brink of being cast aside in favour of a mechanical novelty – the motorcycle. Two bright young men, Bill Harley and Arthur Davidson, were about to make their mark in history as two names upon which the blame for this rested most heavily.

In 1903, Messrs Harley and Davidson joined their surnames to create what was to become the most famous motorcycle marque in the world. The first coupling of the two names was in paint, daubed on the door of a shed in the Davidson family's garden. This was to be the first Harley-Davidson workshop and from it came the first Harley-Davidson motorcycle. In a hundred other garden sheds across the United States, similar hopeful ventures were germinating, but none would become as much a part of the American way of life as

Harley-Davidson. The marque is now the great Californian redwood of motorcycling, a living legend.

Around the year 1900 in America's mid-West, the motorized bicycle was nowhere near being considered a revolution in personal transport. The real revolution was the world-wide boom in pedal cycles. This new and relatively inexpensive form of transport was to many a great sport, and indoor wooden board track racing was hugely popular. The first motorcycles – bicycles with clip-on engines – were built by bicycle

6

manufacturers specifically as race pacers as a means of heading a field of panting competitors – 'breaking the air' as it were – allowing the pedal cyclist to achieve great speeds. Then, however, the concept of the motorized bicycle became established in its own right.

In Milwaukee, Wisconsin, William (Bill) S. Harley and his friend and next-door neighbour Arthur Davidson examined with fascination the efforts of individuals and companies involved in motorizing bicycles. Bill, son of a working-class couple from Manchester, England, and Arthur, son of a cabinet maker from Aberdeen, Scotland, together spent their late teens developing small engines. One of these was put to work powering a rowing boat which belonged to Bill, a keen trout fisherman. As well as fishing, the two men were fanatical cyclists and with their combined interests were all too aware of the potential of the developing relationship between the early petrol engines and pedal cycles. Bill already had considerable mechanical knowledge and aptitude, having worked for two years as an apprentice bicycle fitter in north Milwaukee. He then went on to take another apprenticeship as a draftsman in a metal fabricating plant, the Barth Manufacturing Company, where his school chum Arthur Davidson was an apprentice pattern maker. Their hobby became the petrol engine.

The small clip-on engine at that time used in bicycle racing had its origins in France. It was known as the De Dion-Bouton engine after its inventors, Count Albert de Dion and Georges Bouton, who first fired one into life in 1895. The motor was a simple four-stroke single cylinder petrol engine with an 'atmospheric' inlet valve (the valve was opened and shut merely by the pressure of gas in the cylinder) and was manufactured commercially by the Aster Company of Paris.

During 1900, Harley and Davidson acquired some invaluable material from a work-mate at Barth's, a man named Emil Kroeger. Kroeger was an ex-Aster employee who had emigrated to the burgeoning industrial heartland of the U.S. carrying nothing but a suitcase and a bunch of very interesting blueprints. He had brought with him some original workshop drawings of the small De Dion engine. To two young men who used a lathe for recreation, here was a man who deserved to be bought a drink. In the cold light of day this was in fact a kind of primitive industrial espionage, but who was to know? Paris was a long way from Milwaukee in those days.

With the De Dion design, the partners spent each night after work designing and building their own engine of 2⅛-inch bore and 2⅞-inch stroke based on the drawings. The idea was to fit their engine into a heavyweight pedal cycle frame as a means of propulsion; Harley and Davidson were building a motorcycle!

They experimented for the next two years and were joined in their efforts, part-time, by Arthur's 26 year-old elder brother, Walter, who had been an apprentice machinist for the railroad in Parsons, Kansas. Walter had been kept informed of the friends' progress by letter; detailed, rapturous explanations and descriptions of the motorized bicycle under construction at the Davidson family home at the corner of 38th Street and Highland Avenue, Milwaukee. He was tempted away from his job in Kansas with a promise of a ride on the wonderful new machine. Little did he realize he was expected to help build it first.

With Walter involved part-time (he had found a job at a local railroad company), the project had outgrown the Davidson house and so, with the help of a generous offer from a friend, moved to its own premises, a small basement workshop. It was equipped with a lathe, a drill press and a range of hand tools. In the spring of 1903, the first prototype motorcycle emerged into the light of day.

Road testing began in earnest up, down and around the rutted streets of Milwaukee. It was soon apparent that fitting an engine to a bicycle frame which was only built for the weight and leg power of a human body created destructive stresses beyond acceptability. Besides the broken and distorted frames and wrecked steering head bearings, the motor bicycle's poor 40 kph (25mph) top speed and difficulty in conquering Milwaukee's more demanding gradients meant that a complete reappraisal of the project was necessary.

Firstly, a bigger more powerful engine was needed to push the struggling engineers up the hills. This new motor was Bill Harley's baby (again using the De Dion basic layout, but this time *Bill's* drawings) and had a 3-inch bore and 3½-inch stroke, giving a displacement of 25 cubic inches. It had heavier flywheels and beefier castings. Making the casting patterns was Arthur's job. This was to be the first true Harley-Davidson engine.

The new motor pushed out a mere three horsepower, but this was more than enough to make the pedal-cycle frame redundant. The frame, designed for one-person power, quite simply could no longer handle the greater demands the engine imposed, so a purpose-built chassis was drawn up. This time a loop was built in which to sit the engine, and the diamond shape of the old bicycle was consigned to history. This was the conception of the first ever Harley-Davidson motorcycle to be offered to the public.

Bill Harley and the Davidson brothers were treading new ground with their motorized bicycle, but the real pioneers' footprints were all over the place by the time Arthur and William arrived. Names such as Indian, Excelsior and Pope had been serving the enthusiast market for a few years already. The Harley and Davidson stronger, purpose-built chassis was a direct copy of the best that was around at the time and as already described, their engine was built from French blueprints. They were looking at what was around and used what they saw in their own way with their own solutions. Bill Harley wasn't the most innovative engineer, but he was certainly meticulous. Their wheels, bearings and hubs for the new prototype, for example, were sturdier and stronger than anything else around at the time. They were designed for the heavy job they had to do and to give good service. In building their bikes big, butch and beefy – if lacking new ideas – Bill and Arthur were unwittingly establishing a methodology which would always stay with the Harley-Davidson marque, for good and great success – and also for worse fortune – in the future.

Arthur's cabinet-maker father, William C. Davidson, was right behind the two friend's efforts and ambitions. Aware that Bill and Arthur had created a going concern and needed their own premises, he built a 3 x 4.5 m (10 x 15 ft) workshop in the back garden of the Davidson family house and furnished it with drill press and lathe.

Then came the big question: what would they paint on the door – what ought to be the name of the company? Should it be 'Davidson-Harley' or 'Harley-Davidson'? To modern ears, there is no choice, as the former sounds so clumsy. History records that although the Davidsons outnumbered the Harleys two-to-one in the business and Arthur's dad had built the workshop, 'Harley-Davidson' was voted a smoother couplet for a company name and was also a form of recognition that the team had worked to Bill Harley's original design and concept. Harley Davidson Motor Co, without the

hyphen, was the proud legend printed on the door of the workshop at the rear of 38th St and Highland Avenue, Milwaukee, in the summer of 1903.

Initial production was limited. Two machines were able to be produced over the winter of 1903/4, each financed by the buyer himself, who was required to put down 50 per cent of the purchase price as a deposit, the rest to be paid on delivery. The first bikes were priced at $200, and their sales brochure declared: 'In making our motorcycle, we have not endeavored (sic) to see how cheap we could make it, but how good.' That line would not look out of place in a 1991 sales brochure, although it may have looked far-fetched during some of the darker hours in Harley-Davidson history.

Late in 1903, Bill Harley went back to college at the University of Wisconsin in order to learn more about engineering. If Harley-Davidson was to progress as a company and manufacturer, someone needed to acquire development skills. Bill got a job waiting on tables at a fraternity house to help pay his way. He was to be the only graduate among the founding fathers of Harley-Davidson. The enhanced knowledge of engineering and metallurgy he had gained paid useful dividends later.

The new bike proved reliable – by design and from thorough testing along the rutted dirt roads of Milwaukee. A reliable motorized bicycle was a rarity of the time, due to the quick-buck brigade who were churning out kits and copies of the established marques on the swell of the enthusiast popularity enjoyed by the machines. The Harley-Davidson was built to outlive the fad, and the machine's robust construction showed it. Orders followed quickly.

Arthur's elder brother, Walter, became Harley-Davidson's first full-time employee in the spring of 1904, and work space was doubled.

Four part-time staff were taken on. Arthur was still holding down his 'proper' job, but spent his spare time selling and promoting the still immature marque. Three more bikes were built in 1904, a further five the next year. Harley and the Davidsons were on the brink of something big.

The workshop was too small for production to expand any further, so the Davidsons sought some 'venture capital' from a relative to finance the purchase of land on a Milwaukee industrial estate, conveniently close to the Chicago, Milwaukee and St Paul Railroad. The plot was on the corner of 27th Street and Chestnut Street which would later become Juneau Avenue – the present address of Harley-Davidson International.

Initially it was not the most substantial of structures, as Walter Davidson is recorded as saying: 'After we had the framework up, the railroad surveyors notified us that we were encroaching on the right of way of the adjacent railroad. So we got about eight or ten fellows, picked up the entire shop and moved it back about a foot and a half, so that we were safe.' The new premises allowed expansion of production to almost one machine a week during 1906. Arthur finally joined the company full time, leaving his job as a pattern maker forever, in order to devote his life to the manufacture and sale of Harley-Davidson motorcycles. Sales trebled to a previously unimaginable 152 machines during 1907, thanks to Arthur's enfranchisement of a number of local bicycle dealers.

Indeed, the bicycle dealers formed the network which would take Harley-Davidson to the public, in the way it had for George M. Hendee with the Indian motorcycle and the George N. Pierce Company with the Pope, two great marques of the era. Arthur Davidson, whose role in the business since 1904 had been the promotion and sale of the machines, took special care that those he granted dealerships were well-versed in the maintenance and repair of his company's product. In 1907, the Harley-Davidson marque scored a contractual coup by supplying the police department with machines, so creating the first Harley-mounted patrolmen.

Once a limited dealer network was established, the next logical step was to establish Harley-Davidson formally, by incorporating the partnership as a company under state law. The Harley-Davidson Motor Company of Milwaukee became a legal corporate identity on 22 September, 1907. Walter Davidson was its first President and General Manager, his brother Arthur was nominated General Sales Manager and Company Secretary, and William S. Harley, as yet an undergraduate, was given the role and title of Chief Engineer and Designer. The shares were bought by all 17 of the company's employees, and the capital was ploughed back in to enable the company to expand.

At the same time, a third Davidson, William A., the eldest brother at 36 years, joined the company as Vice President and Works Manager. As well as strengthening the family control of the enterprise, he was a perfect addition to the team, leaving the Chicago, Milwaukee and St Paul Railroad repair shop where he had learned his trade as a toolmaker and fabricator and worked as shop foreman. Harley-Davidson was now established, and the company got down to business with gusto.

SILENCE IS GRAY
By 1908, Harley-Davidson, along with around three dozen other manufacturers, were giving the United States what it wanted – mobility on a budget – in the dawn of an age which was witnessing Henry Ford's vision of mass-produced, all-black, horseless carriages. Harley-Davidson were

Harley-Davidson's first full production motorcycle – the 35 cu inch Silent Gray Fellow.

doing their bit to fill the gap with an all-grey vision – their first production model whose sober dress and whispering presence earned it respect among the public and the nickname, the *Silent Gray Fellow*.

In their first decade of life, motorcycles were already gaining a notoriety for their anti-social traits. Manufacturers and owners enjoyed advertising their modernity with open exhausts much to the distress of other street users and especially those involved in pulling carriages. The horse was still king, albeit at the end of his rein!

The Harley-Davidson Motor Company's first policy was to keep its product sociable by fitting large silencers to even their earliest models, hence the *Silent* part of the early model's nickname. The *Gray*? Well, that was the standard colour offered by the company after the

first handful of black bikes that formed their first two years' production. Flying in the face of Fordism, black was no option. The *Fellow* part of the nickname is of psychological as well as historical interest. It seems from their very beginnings, Harley-Davidson motorcycles have been blessed with that intangible asset of 'character', which owners would come to recognize and become attached to.

The first Harley-Davidson full production engine, as fitted to the Silent Gray Fellow was based on the De Dion, but differed in the following respects. It had a larger bore and stroke, 3 x 3½ inches, which gave 3hp potential, and the flywheel had virtually doubled in diameter, to 11½ inches. Instead of the 'atmospheric' valves of the De Dion, this motor featured side pocket valves. It also had large cooling fins on the cylinder and head.

To the historical eye, the second prototype in production from 1904 was still more bicycle-boneshaker than motorbike, with no suspension front or rear as such. It was built of much heavier gauge tubing however, and the forks and steering head bearings had been strengthened where forces had proved so damaging in the first prototype. The wheelbase was lengthened by the provision of more generous accommodation for the motor, giving the bike better stability.

Drive to the back wheel was via a leather belt, which was tensioned to give traction using a spring-loaded pulley and hand lever; it doubled as a clutch when temporary stops were needed. The design was so simple you could see how it worked just by looking. Starting the bike was not that far removed from the frantic and ungraceful efforts employed by step-thru moped riders of just a few years ago, involving some serious leg-work until the engine could be brought up to pace. Drive could be engaged by gradually tensioning the leather

belt on its bottom run until the motor was under full load. A true clutch with friction plates allowing a gradual engagement of drive had yet to be thought of, and so use of a chain and toothed sprocket for drive was difficult without it. Such a bike would have two speeds – go and stop. Belt drive gave at least some control over speed, as it had the facility to slip the drive belt around the drive pulley, by slackening the tensioner. It had its drawbacks, mainly that it slipped uncontrollably in wet weather.

While at university, Harley came up with a solution to the necessarily violent behaviour of their bike's rigid front end – a suspension system which was to stay with the company for some 40 years, before it was superseded by telescopic forks. Who could have foreseen its reintroduction some *80 years* later in one of the most outrageous marketing ploys in motorcycle history. The irony is, although the system was used on subsequent generations of Harley-Davidsons and was used on many makes of motorcycle worldwide, it

The Silent Gray Fellow – this particular bike first hit the dusty roads of Milwaukee in 1912.

was never particularly efficient, giving increasingly unpredictable handling as the performance of the engines outpaced their capabilities.

Essentially, William came up with the leading link principle. This involved an unsprung fork and a sprung fork set in front of it. The sprung fork moved up and down, the unsprung fork was fixed. A pivoting link attached the two sets of fork legs at the bottom and the wheel axle ran through the forward sprung fork. The sprung leading link forks had their advantages over and above the ability to absorb a bump in the road; they were very rigid and strong and at the levels of performance the 1904 engine provided, were very fit for the job. They were soon incorporated into the design of the Silent Gray Fellow.

The durability of Harley-Davidson motorcycles was established from the earliest years,

indeed the earliest sale proved to be the model example for the future. The first production bike was sold to a Mr Meyer who rode it for 9,650 km (6,000 miles). He sold it to George Lyon, who managed an impressive 24,100 km (15,000 miles). It passed through the hands of three other owners, who together totted up a further 99,800 km (62,000 miles). In 1913, the factory, which still had contact with the whereabouts of their very first production machine, proudly announced that it had covered 160,900 km (100,000 miles) with no major component or bearing needing replacement.

The larger premises and land at Chestnut Street allowed production to leap to 49 machines during 1906. Five extra workhands were taken on to cope with the increased demand. The following year the company was incorporated, the shares being divided among the families and employees. Over the next three years there was a virtual explosion of popularity for the Harley-Davidson motorcycle, with

production tripling year on year, until by 1910 over 3,000 bikes per annum were coming out of the factory, which had during this time expanded physically to cope. With Bill Harley returning from Wisconsin University with his BSc degree in engineering, it was time for a new model to be introduced.

THE V-TWIN ENGINE
The first thing Bill Harley (BSc Auto Eng) undertook on his return home from college in 1908 was the redesign of the existing model which had served for five years, largely undeveloped. A new engine was mapped out, the same configuration – a pocket valve exhaust, atmospheric intake valve, single cylinder – but this time with a larger displacement of 35 cu inches. Bore and stroke were both increased to 3⁵⁄₁₆ inches x 4 inches. The new model was to be called the 5-35, the 5 referring to the machine's power output, 5 hp, and

The Harley-Davidson 11 hp V-twin or 60.34 cu inch of 1915 has a three-speed gear box. This bike was known as an Eleven F, and when new, cost $275. It became famous for its strength, reliability and speed.

the 35 referring to the cubic capacity in inches.

To handle the extra power, the frame was strengthened and elongated to assist stability. The wheelbase went out from 51 inches to 57 inches. This was a bike capable of up to 80 kph (50mph), so its dependable handling was of paramount importance. The model was to stay in production until 1918, but it was about to be overshadowed by a truly momentous new development which would set the course of Harley-Davidson from then until the present day and beyond – this was the V-twin engine.

Out of historical perspective, the development of the V-twin was a rather logical and unimaginative

step for Harley-Davidson. Everyone was doing it. Adding another cylinder was the simplest and most expedient route to more power, without the necessity of a large amount of redesigning, adding much weight or calling for a new chassis. Power could, in fact, be doubled and, more importantly the V-twin gave exceptional torque characteristics at low revolutions. Besides, a V-configuration fitted perfectly into those old bicycle frames.

These positive characteristics aside, the narrow-angle V-twin was not, nor is it today for that matter, a particularly good configuration for a motorcycle engine. Firstly, with the cylinders set at 45° to one another, the engine is not in primary balance (i.e. the inertial forces of the pistons do not cancel out each other), as is say a 90° V-twin or a flat twin. This means the engine suffers incurable vibration. Furthermore, if more power is sought from a bigger displacement,

11

Below: Harley-Davidson V-twin bore 84.1 mm stroke 88.9 mm 988.83 cm.

Above: Harley-Davidson gasoline tank – main capacity tank 11½ pints, emergency reserve tank 3½ pints.

Below: Brown Speedometer of New Britain, Connecticut. Photograph of drive from rear wheel.

Above: Double stem cushion fork front suspension.

Below: Below the tool box is the sliding gear transmission by Harley-Davidson.

The first V-twin – the 61. This is an X8E from 1914, featuring Bill Harley's own design clutch – an innovation of its time.

the closeness of the cylinders precludes boring the cylinder out – the crank has to be stroked to give more cubes. As all motors coming out of Japan these days demonstrate, oversquare (bore larger than stroke) engines make for higher revving and more powerful engines. Thus the big V-twin's piston speed is limited, which means the engine, in practise, isn't safe to rev over 7,000rpm without being in danger of shaking itself to pieces. This holds true even today in our era of high technology.

Despite everything, the V-twin survives as the central theme of Harley-Davidson motorcycles to the present day, indeed the V-twin

and Harley have become almost synonymous. Any Japanese V-twin is inevitably labelled a Harley-Davidson copy. Fortunately, a satisfyingly 'torquey', simple motor still finds friends among motorcyclists, no matter what the engineering or oriental trends.

Returning to the past, the V-twin was considered an unqualified good move. The Silent Gray Fellow had won the trust and hearts of so many, that there was no point in jeopardizing its reputation by attempting to boost its power still further at the possible expense of reliability, until then the foundation of the Harley-Davidson success. No, a new engine was the way forward.

In 1909, Harley-Davidson's second model, the Sixty-One, appeared. Here was the shape of all things to come. The number referred to the engine's cubic inch

capacity, and the engine produced 7 hp, some 4 hp more than the single cylinder bike. The machine's top speed was a creditable 97 kph (50 mph) and considering the state of roads at that time, it would be safe to assume that this was exciting enough for anyone. During 1909, the factory produced 27 twins. It was, however, a failure because of the unsuitability of the atmospheric intake valve which worked on a single, but not on a twin.

In 1910, the Harley-Davidson Motor Co was an 860 m² (9,250 sq ft) concrete building housing 149 workers. Production that year was 3,200 motorcycles. None of these was the new twin however. Bill Harley eventually adopted the use of the mechanical intake valve, or pocket-valve, which was almost the last obstacle in the way of the machine's mass production.

By 1912, Bill Harley had recognized that the chain drive was the only way to go (a slight irony in view of Harley-Davidson's modern application of toothed belt drive to nearly all its models). He held off, however, until he had a sensible solution for engagement of drive: a clutch. No chain-driven bike produced at the time had a practical method of disengaging the engine when drawing to a halt. Bill came up with one, and fitted it to his 1912 model, the X8E. It was the first properly functioning and commercially acceptable clutch to be used on a motorcycle and it allowed Bill Harley to use the roller chain he knew to be a superior means of driving the bike.

The clutch was a big hit, especially in commercial use, making it a most manageable machine when stop-starting among traffic. Another innovation that year enhanced the big V's attraction still further: the 'Ful-Floteing' seat. As described, the front forks were now sprung, but the rear end of the bikes of the day were still rigid, with obvious detriment to the rider's rear end. Bill Harley's answer was a spring-loaded saddle – a 36-cm (14-inch) spring supporting the seat tube. Harley-Davidson were demonstrating a gentle and acceptable side of motorcycling. It

could not fail to bring them commercial success.

The name Harley-Davidson was spreading across the United States, not only because of the machine's famous reliability, but also through sporting success. From the inception of the first model, folk were entering the bikes in races – endurance trials, board track races and dirt track oval sprints. Harley and Davidson had no initial interest in such ventures and unlike other factories of the era, had no factory riders.

In 1908, however, Walter Davidson couldn't resist entering the Silent Gray Fellow in the Catskill Mountains of New York Endurance Run. It was the only Harley-Davidson among 65 entrants riding 17 different makes of motorcycle. The riders faced a two-day slog over 587 km (365 miles) of rough terrain. After day one, only 43 competitors remained in the trial, which then began a 306 km (190 miles) lap of Long Island. Walter won. He is reported to have commented afterwards: 'So strong was my confidence that I carried with me no additional parts or repairs which was quite in contrast with many of the manufacturers' riders who had automobiles with complete duplicate parts following them.'

This was victory enough for Harley-Davidson, and they left the privateer to prove the worth of their machines in out-and-out racing events. Walter continued to enter occasional endurance trials more with the intention of establishing a reputation for reliability for Harley-Davidson than to fill a room with trophies. It was a useful marketing exercise. This attitude could not be sustained indefinitely, however, especially as it seemed the motorcycle-buying public's imagination was hooked on motorcycle sport. Huge crowds were attending events. By 1913, the factory finally came round to recognizing the validity of racing as part of their marketing strategy.

A particularly well-publicized defeat highlighted certain deficiencies in the Harley-Davidson machinery, namely its lack of power and its one-speed gearing. The event was a desert road race of 716 gruelling kilometres (445 miles) over North America's worst roads from San Diego, California to Phoenix, Arizona. Two privately entered Harleys trundled in to finish last. It was the norm for private entrants to receive factory support for the consumables, and one of the competitors publicly denounced President Walter Davidson for being 'too tight-fisted to even offer to pay for fuel, oil and tyres'.

Meanwhile in the motorcycle press, Harley-Davidson advertisements read 'Don't blame us when Harley-Davidson wins a race meet, because we do not believe in racing. We do not employ any racing men. We build no special racing machines, but the results speak for themselves.' Harley-Davidson were proclaiming that they didn't believe in racing and were capitalizing on it in the same breath. Such blatant hypocrisy upset many Harley-Davidson sporting enthusiasts, and the Harley-Davidson board realized it was skating on thin ice.

In late 1913, in a move which officially recognized the value of sporting achievements in marketing their bikes, Harley-Davidson secured the appointment of Bill Ottaway, an engineer of imagination and flair, who had been responsible for the particularly fast Thor racing motorcycles. Bill Harley was to continue as Chief Engineer and in his own particular, methodical way, turned his attention to designing a gearbox. The board ensured Ottaway was well aware that he was

expected to work only within the existing engine configuration rather than to design anything radically different. This early display of commercial restraint has been a hallmark of Harley-Davidson Motor Co throughout its entire history, right to the present day.

Ottaway began developing the twin, for more power and less vibration, and set up Harley-Davidson's first Race Department. Ottaway's efforts resulted in a 129 kph (80mph) rocketship with a

chassis that could barely contain the power. In 1914 Harley-Davidson took the win at the Birmingham, Alabama One-Hour National Championship; in 1915 a further 26 major wins were attributed to the marque. It was a force to be reckoned with. Now before Harley-Davidson there stretched a glorious racing future.

This original Eleven F has been beautifully restored by the owner, Shaun Baker of Somerset, England.

From War to Depression

Harley-Davidson's infant years had been a period of dynamic expansion. It had reached a point, just prior to the outbreak of World War I in 1914, where nothing could be envisaged or expected but healthy growth on the solid foundations the prudent founding fathers had laid down. When war did come for the United States in 1917, history records that the fire that had razed Europe and consumed its young men in their

hundreds of thousands, was burning itself out. American military might poured in and finally quenched those flames. It was a devastating war for Europe, but little felt across the Atlantic divide. The United States' war effort until then had been

An example of the 74 J from 1927. Sales literature of the time promoted it as the 'stream-line Harley', and it became known as the Streamliner.

primarily material support for the Allied military.

By the end of the war in 1918, 316 of Harley's work-force were involved in military service. Of those who went overseas, three did not return. The Harley production lines in Milwaukee had assembled 20,000 bikes specifically destined for military action. Turning production over from civilian to military involved little more than a change of colour in the paintshop

THE KNUCKLEHEAD
This is the type '61' overhead valve V-twin engine of 61 cu inches (999 cc), the first Harley-Davidson to have a circulating pressure oiling system. This pressure system was unreliable in 1936, when it was launched, but by 1937 it had been modified.

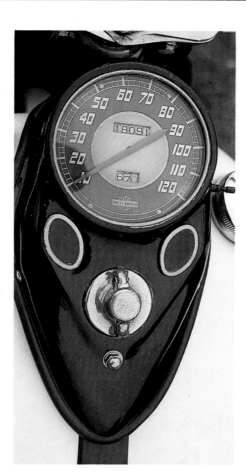

Left: The 120 mph Harley-Davidson speedometer on the 1939 EL Sports Solo. There is a trip lever on the right and chrome ignition switch below.

Below: The Knucklehead shown here is a 1939 model EL Sports Solo.

from the standard grey to military green. Readjusting after the war was not exactly an upheaval: Harley-Davidson retained green as standard in the post-war years, adjusting the shade to a subdued olive green.

As ever, the board had kept their commitment to the war effort within reason, in contrast to the Indian motorcycle factory which had been pumping out cut-price military machinery almost

exclusively – to the chagrin and detriment of their dealer network throughout the country. Harley-Davidson, with a typically longer-sighted approach, had been battling on both fronts, splitting its 17,000 units for 1916/17 marginally in favour of the civilian market. Then, as the conflict ended, it was Harley-Davidson who inadvertently scored a great public relations coup by carrying the first American, Corporal Roy Holtz, on

today. Ricardo was engaged in order to help develop the Ottaway's II-K racing model 61 engine which now featured four valves per cylinder. His efforts yielded an engine producing an astounding 55 hp – in 1915! Harleys greatest wartime victories were destined to be on the tracks. Their race-team earned the nickname the *Wrecking Crew* and they toured the United States, taking win after win, record after record, on their eight-valve 160 kph+ (100 mph+) machines.

Harley's war efforts were concentrated on one model, the 61 'J', which was gradually refined to become a well-equipped (with battery and generator), high-quality machine. With the war behind them, and their world position considerably strengthened, Harley-Davidson expanded their production capabilities by 100 per cent, investing $3.5 million in a new works and tooling.

In 1919, after dropping production of the single, they shocked the industry by introducing a new model to fill a perceived gap in the market for a middleweight, gentleman's machine. The W Sport Twin was a shameless copy of the English Douglas, a flat-twin laid 'fore and aft' in the frame, of 37 cu inches (600cc) and 6 hp. It had a three-speed gearbox, a multiplate clutch in an oil-bath and an enclosed final drive chain; there was even an option with battery, coil and electric lights. It was truly a format designed to carry the factory for many years.

However, the new machine, with all its promise, flopped. Despite heavy promotion, the American public was too besotted with the V-twin, for all its vibration and foibles, to accept this radical

one of their bikes, into the defeated Germany before the war reporters' cameras.

The war effort opened another door for Harley-Davidson – the export market. Harley-Davidson had become international. Britain, the primary source of European motorcycles, had been churning out guns in favour of bikes for four years, and the American marques had filled the gap in the market. Indeed, Harley-Davidson had

created a 2,000-strong dealer network which reached every civilized country accounting for 15 per cent of production.

While the world immersed itself in conflict, motorcycle development continued undisturbed in the United States. During the war years, Ottaway talked Walter Davidson into shipping over Harry Ricardo, a leading English engine expert whose company remains so even

The Knucklehead was the first OHV motorcycle to be built in the United States. It could produce a speed of over 145 kph (90 mph).

configuration. Furthermore, it offered little potential for development. It was rejected by the public and after four years, by a sheepish Harley factory.

THE ROARING TWENTIES
Harley-Davidson entered the new decade with a factory covering 37,200 m² (400,000 sq ft), a work-force of 1,800 and a production capacity of 70,000 motorcycles a year. Just as with every other American manufacturer, however, for Harley the 1920s didn't roar at all. It was a period of decline and gloom for the two-wheelers. The popular 'J' model was to carry the factory through the lean years and as if responding to the austere

atmosphere in the market, Harley-Davidson launched two 21 cu inch (350cc) single-cylinder models, the 'Peashooters' as they were dubbed by cynical dealers and punters. Scathing they might be, but the model would find great success in export markets and endure in the United States to become a showroom success as well as a racing success.

Henry Ford was perhaps the main enemy of the American motorcycle industry in the early 1920s. His revolutionary production line methods flooded the United States with affordable black Model Ts. His lead was followed by competing automobile manufacturers. Harley production had dropped to the lowest for ten years – 10,000. The motorcycle was being run off the roads of America.

By 1922, these dire market conditions forced two enemy camps

to sit together, smoke the peace-pipe and try to powwow themselves out of trouble. Harley-Davidson and Indian agreed a price-fixing strategy to avoid their mutual destruction in the face of a common enemy. The compact agreed, Harley-Davidson went away and launched a direct competitor to Indian's top of the range *Big Chief*. Designated the '74', it was a 1200 cc capacity heavyweight which won instant popularity.

In 1923, the factory suspended its racing programme, viewing it as an unnecessary overhead, for the time being anyway. The market was bleak. As a gauge of the threat the Ford's automobiles posed the motorcycle industry during the 1920s: in 1924 a basic Model T retailed for $265; a Harley 74 in 1926 was priced at $325. In effect, this meant the car had superseded

19

the motorcycle as a utilitarian vehicle, pushing the latter into the position of a leisure item, and a much more precarious existence.

Harley survived these lean years by eking out the life of the 'J' model. They ended the decade on a high note with a best-seller launched in 1928. The twin-cam JD61 and JDH74, were two superb, though expensive, machines and represent the zenith of 'J' development. Besides offering great tuning potential, they featured an innovation, for Harley, which was received with a curious scepticism by the rider of the day. They had front brakes.

THE GREAT DEPRESSION

Pushing a miserable decade behind them, and heartened by an upturn in sales in 1929, the industry's best year since 1919, Harley launched three new models in late 1929 – just as the stock market crashed. Although it would take a year for the Great Depression to become entrenched, in these three new bikes, Harley had created more immediate problems.

In a fever of rationalization at the factory, two of the new models, a 45 cu-inch (750 cc) V-twin and a 30.5 cu-inch (500 cc) single, were given the same chassis. The 45 was to prove a classic, a reliable and trustworthy workhorse which would continue in production into the 1950s. However, its introduction to the public was an unqualified disaster. The new twin and the single were presented without adequate prototype testing, and without consideration of their positions in the market.

The 45 proved slow – very slow – and offered no alternative benefits over the new single, itself encumbered by an over-engineered chassis. In compromising the chassis to accept either of the two motors, the designers had left no room for the twin's generator, which ended up clumsily placed vertically alongside the front cylinder. The wags soon dubbed it the 'three-cylinder Harley'.

If its looks and poor speed were not enough, the new 45 had mechanical trouble too. The generator drive shaft was a new component to facilitate the generator's odd positioning and turned out to be prone to disintegration under load. Inundated with complaints, the factory produced a carb kit to boost power and an improved drive shaft for the generator. The single fared little better, its gross chassis causing too much stress for the lightweight engine, leading to piston failure.

As if to rub Harley-Davidson's nose in it, Excelsior, the third major American manufacturer, launched a 45 at the same time – with a real beauty of an engine. It was an ironic slap in the face for Harley-Davidson, as it had been designed by Arthur Constantine in 1925, just before he got the sack from Walter Davidson. Excelsior, his new employer, realized the design. The 145 kph (90 mph) Super X, as it was named, even outclassed the 101 Indian Scout, a machine capable of a creditable 129 kph (80 mph).

The third new model hardly redeemed the freshly beleaguered factory. It was a monster. Forty-five kg (100 lb) heavier than the 'J', it weighed in at 249 kg (550 lb) all-up. The bike, designated the VL, was a 1200 cc side-valve engine claiming 27 bhp. The side valves, as fitted to the 45, seemed to be a step backward, as was the total loss lubrication system. However, there were many positive aspects to using side valves: it meant much cheaper detachable cylinder heads could be used, maintenance was easier and, besides, Indian had shown the system to be wholly acceptable to the public. Harley were playing safe – or so they thought.

The VL had incorporated into it a serious design flaw: the crank flywheels were too small. The idea had been to make a free-revving responsive engine, possibly with juicy police department contracts in mind. Spritely it was, but only up to about 80 kph (50 mph). Thereafter, the power evaporated and the most horrendous vibration set in, blurring vision and chattering teeth. The dealers revolted; the factory panicked. Orders were cancelled, bikes returned.

Bill Harley and the engineering department locked themselves in the workshop until they found an answer. It was a virtual redesign. Larger flywheels meant a larger crankcase; larger crankcases meant a redesigned frame to accommodate it. The cam and valves were made more radical to give the bike more poke. The new frames and cranks and cases (what else was there left?) were issued to dealers, who collectively redressed over 1,300 claims, paying labour costs themselves. It cost Harley-Davidson and their dealers a fortune. Many of the latter threw back their franchises to the company's face.

The early 1930s brought world economic and social catastrophe. No-one escaped. The American motorcycle industry was ostensibly trying to help itself with its annual, and illegal, price-fixing meetings. Behind the scenes, Harley-Davidson was conducting a despicable business policy of 'dog-eat-dog' for which they later apologized and ate humble pie before tycoon E. Paul du Pont, a new and major shareholder in Indian. At the price-fixing meeting of 1932, du Pont called upon Arthur Davidson to explain why his agents were pushing out VL police specials to forces at virtually cost price and scrapping non-Harley makes taken in part exchange. It was a shameful episode and a demonstration of the Harley-Davidson executives' paranoia about, and hatred of, competing makes.

It was a time of desperate measures, however. Harley's worst year in ten, 1933 was a far cry from the boom year of 1929. Sales nation-wide stood at 6,000; Harley-Davidson secured 3,700. The 1932 price-fixing meeting set retail prices at rock-bottom for both Indian and Harley Davidson. Since the advent of the cheap automobile, motorcycles had become luxury items, and in hard times were the first to suffer. The Depression hit the car market almost as badly – second-hand Model Ts were virtually worthless, as one-third of America's working population became idle. Thousands of banks failed, taking with them the life savings of so many; a third of the railroad companies, a mainstay of employment in the young nation, went broke. Harley kept its work-force intact by work-sharing rather than laying off.

In view of the motorcycle's increasingly luxury-market image, Harley-Davidson introduced their first factory 'custom' options in 1933, switching from the olive green to bright colour options and Art Deco style motifs. For $15 extra, the customer could opt for a fully-chromed bike. The initially disastrous and clumsy VL had been accepted with time and the factory began again with the 45, and by 1932 had created an acceptable machine. That same year the Servi-Car was introduced, in the hope that the Harley wasn't just a gentleman's toy. Their hopes were fulfilled. This strange incarnation of a Harley – a three-wheeler 'delivery van' – was to continue in production until 1974!

By 1934 Harley-Davidson was recovering from the Great Depression, with a healthy upturn in sales to around 10,000. The world economy had bottomed out, the United States was emerging from depression, and a new Presidential reign had begun with Franklin Delano Roosevelt's socialist-influenced 'New Deal', a programme designed to protect Americans from the harder edge of capitalism. At the Juneau Avenue works, drawing boards were dusted

off and plans laid for a model whose close derivatives would carry Harley-Davidson through the next 50 years and compound for the marque its legendary status. The model was to be christened the *Knucklehead.*

The new model was officially designated the 61E – the factory since the earliest days of the Silent Gray Fellow had left it to the dealers and enthusiasts to title their models for them. Its basic engine and frame design endures to the present day as a dry sump lubricated overhead-valve motor (marking the end of total loss lubrication), and four-speed constant mesh gearbox housed in a double cradle frame. It was the lumpy-shaped rocker covers atop the engine which gave the bike its *Knucklehead* tag. It was the first OHV motorcycle to be built in the United States. The real value of the overhead valves, though, was the increased power output they gave the 1,000 cc engine which could push the 272 kg (600 lb) beast to over 145kph (90 mph).

It seems, sadly, that the Harley-Davidson executive learned little from their mistakes. The 61E, like the original 45 and VL, were shipped out to an eager public with insufficient prototype development under its belt. Amazingly it was a problem as obvious as a propensity to leak oil from the all new top-end which was allowed to slip by and into production.

Again, the midnight oil was burned in the engineering department; again the dealers and first 1,900 owners were faced with potential breakdown; again a kit was distributed to put the matter right. In an effort to divert attention from its more negative attributes, the new model was the subject of a publicity stunt to achieve a world 'ocean-sand' record, which still stands today. The famous Joe Petrali made a speed run on Daytona's beach, and the bike scored a flying mile of 136.18 mph average, beating by

10 mph the existing record set on an Indian in 1932.

Following the 61E came two new models, built in the old mould – side-valve engines of 74 and 80 cu inches, designated the UL and the ULH. They had similar chassis to the Knucklehead, and dry sump, circulated lubrication. Although bulky at more than 272 kg (600 lb), they were a hit from the start, thanks to their sheer ruggedness, grunty 30 hp engine, their ease of maintenance and reliability. Perfect for sidecars, perfect for touring, perfect for police forces. Each bike's longevity as a model was limited by the growing interest in the Knucklehead and its successors. It was with this overhead valve design where Harley-Davidson's future would lie.

With the sporty 61E Knucklehead, the two U models were the ideal complement to the new Harley line-up. These models replaced the 74 VL, a model which had earned a degree of respect after a shaky introduction. The sidevalve 45, introduced at the same time as the 74 VL remained in production and would continue right up till 1952. The engine would hang on in, housed in the Servi-Car until 1974! The single-cylinder bikes, the 30.5-inch *Baby Harley* and the 21-inch *Peashooter* both went out of production in 1934.

As a new era began in Harley-Davidson hardware, an era ended as one of its founders passed on. William A. Davidson died in 1937. William A. was the eldest brother and had joined the company in 1907 as Vice President and Works Manager at the age of 36; his expertise was in manufacturing techniques learned from 20 years with the railroad. His tool-making skills meant the factory could produce just about all its bikes' component parts – from nuts and bolts to the enormous hundred-ton press which stamped out the tanks and fenders. This self-sufficiency is a virtue which the company has stayed with to the present day.

Harley-Davidson Goes to War

In Europe war was raging. The many and varied countries which occupied a body of land small enough to fit inside Texas were in the midst of a fight to death. The world had shrunk since the Great War too, and this new conflict would not be contained. Americans were more uneasy now, as the war in Europe became a truly global affair, drawing in all nations

around the world, including those on their doorstep, the Japanese and the Russians. U-boats prowled every ocean, no target was too far for the bombers. It was an impossible war for the United States to stay out of and the Axis

This example of model WLA is to full combat specification, as detailed opposite.

powers knew it, pre-empting America's commitment by attacking Pearl Harbor on December 7, 1941. There was no executive decision for President Franklin D. Roosevelt to make. Emperor Hirohito of Japan had already made it for him.

During the war, Harley-Davidson played their own vital role, providing transport for Allied

Detail of rear carrier and leather bags.

The WLA - detail

> **MODEL WLA 1942**
> *1942 saw the United States fully into World War II. Some 90,000 WLA and WLC model Harley-Davidsons were produced for communication, scouting and military police duties. The WLC model was built to Canadian government specification and supplied to the Canadian and Allied armies.*
>
> *The full WLA combat specification included front fork mounted Thompson SMG holster and ammunition box, rear carrier and leather bags, transmission and engine sump guard (skid-tray), front and rear blackout lamps, oil bath air filter, windshield assembly and leg shields.*
>
> *The WLA was gradually replaced by the jeep, which was more suited to the fighting terrain in Europe, but it was still retained for scouting in advance of U.S. Armored Divisions. During the advance through Holland, it became affectionately known as the 'Liberator' because the Harley and its rider were usually the first Allied troops to make contact with the local population.*
>
> *The WLA, with slight modifications, continued to be produced in limited numbers for the U.S. forces into the early 1950s.*
>
> *The motorcycle shown here has identification markings for U.S. army, 2nd Armored Division (Hell-on-Wheels), Police Detachment, HQ Company, 5th Vehicle in Troop.*
> **TECHNICAL SPECIFICATION**
> *Rigid frame, chain drive, solo motorcycle, V-twin, 750 cc. Three-speed transmission, tank mounted, hand gear change with foot operated clutch.*
> *Top speed in military service 105 kph (65 mph).*

troops at every battle site in the world, spreading their name, enhancing their reputation and securing a lasting place in the affections of every soldier who was detailed to ride one. Harley-Davidson: the soldier's friend. During the war, thousands of GIs would be taught to ride, maintain – and love – motorcycles, and they would bring their new passion back home with them, for good and for worse.

The war not only brought with it a heightening of American awareness of motorcycling and the Harley-Davidson, but an international familiarity with the marque too. There was not one country in the conflict left untouched by Harley-Davidson, creating an interest in and loyalty to the marque which would strengthen Harley-Davidson's international position in peacetime.

President Roosevelt had warned the United States to steel itself for

what was to come as war was declared in Europe in 1939. The two American giants, Harley-Davidson and Indian, received their call-up papers in the autumn of that same year, not because the United States was beginning to stockpile, but because the West Midlands of England, where most of the world's motorcycles were produced had been all but obliterated by the Luftwaffe as their first port of call. Britain ordered 5,000 bikes from each American factory.

The specification for such machines had, as top priority, reliability and ruggedness, and Harley had just the machine in the 45 cu-inch (750 cc) D model, which would be beefed-up for the job. This was the side-valve model that had begun life in 1929 as an underpowered, undependable heap which arrived at the Harley-Davidson dealers with a power-up kit and had its frame and motor totally revised within the year. By

1939, however, all bugs had been removed and the 45 had several years of reliable service to its credit and had gained a reputation for an almost-indestructible gearbox and clutch and good torque characteristics, although with little top-end speed.

The army's mount was designated the WLA (the A standing for 'army'), painted GI olive green drab and in anticipation of gruelling duties ahead, was given 18-inch wheels and 4½-inch section wheels, knobbly tyres, raised mudguards and a steel 'sump' guard. The engine was 'detuned' somewhat by lowering the compression ratio, and its longevity addressed by extending the cylinders' and heads' cooling fins and fitting a large air filter. It was now capable of only about 80 kph (50 mph), but retained its 'torquey' pulling power, which would certainly be its greatest asset. This bike would have to cope with the frozen mud of the Russian Steppes and the shifting sands of the North African desert alike.

The WLA model accounted for virtually all the factory's wartime production, totalling a staggering 88,000 bikes during the five-year run; the Soviet army used two thirds of this number in their push from the east toward Berlin – a cavalry of Harleys.

Late in 1942, the U.S. Army Procurement Department issued a rather insulting order to both the Indian and Harley-Davidson factory. They were told to produce machines based on the German BMW horizontally-opposed flat-twin design (which endures today). Swallowing their pride for the all-American V-twin, the two factories set about designing flat-twin models with which Rommel had so impressed the struggling Allies.

Harley-Davidson came up with a 45 cu inch (750 cc) sidevalve machine, designated the XA. It was specified to have shaft-drive, a benefit the BMWs enjoyed in the

Above: The owner of this bike is Iain Cottrell, who specializes in the restoration of ex-military Harleys for both museums and private collectors throughout the world. Cottrell is based in Weymouth, England.

Left: WLA with the 'Hell-on-Wheels' identification markings.

abrasive conditions of the desert. Harley chains and sprockets were soon worn to nothing in the sand. Furthermore, the XA model boasted a hand-operated clutch and four-speed gearbox operated by foot lever; Harley's Vs were still hand shift with foot-operated clutch and three-speed transmission. The XA was setting the trend for Harley's future.

The model itself promised long, dependable service as a pure workhorse, but the first examples were marred (to no-one's great surprise) by valve gear weakness and lubrication problems. They were teething troubles which would never be addressed, as by the time the first 1,000 had been produced, the war in North Africa was at an end and the XA was redundant.

With such a prolific output during the war years, one would imagine Harley-Davidson had been one of the few beneficiaries of the period. In a general sense, they had benefitted by the dissemination of their bikes throughout the world, but in hard cash terms, their war effort had been unremunerative. Harley-Davidson had been dealing on a cost plus 10 per cent basis with the Forces. Furthermore, there was no winding down of production toward the end of the war; it just ended, with all contracts being cancelled early in 1944. This left the Juneau Avenue stores department with enough components to assemble 30,000 WLA machines from spare parts.

Army surplus became big business, not just with the factory in Milwaukee. Mr Norman Holliday, a close family friend of the author, had been stationed in India with the Royal Air Force just after the war. He was posted to an abandoned U.S. airfield, where he and his colleagues found two aircraft hangars, each stacked to the ceiling, one with refrigerators, and the other with GI Indian 741s, still in their packing cases. It was their job to dispose of any abandoned equipment as they saw fit.

The Indian motorcycles were fitted with machine gun mounts and many a boring afternoon was lightened by trips up and down the runways, throttle to the stop, riddling with bullets the hapless vultures and buzzards which lived (and died) around the airfield. The bikes and refrigerators, which officially did not exist, would also be sold to any local who could scrape together enough cigarettes

or liquor to impress the soldiers. In such a poor underdeveloped country, both were powerful status symbols.

With a careless disregard for human life, the aircraftsmen would hand over the bikes to the eager punters, many of whom spoke only odd words of English. They'd be given 1 pint of petrol and two minutes instruction of how to start and ride the machine, much of which (including crucial stopping procedures) would go straight over the politely nodding heads of the keen would-be motorcyclists. They would wobble off the airfield and up the dusty road, many to oblivion. Our old friend Mr Holliday would recount (with a poker face) how each proud new

owner would be accompanied by two or three hopeful vultures which would follow his erratic progress from on high.

At about the same time, around 15,000 Harley WLAs and 6,000 Indian 741s were sold off by the United States government to the civilian market, both in the U.S. and England. The price was $450 and although expensive in relation to the unofficial deals going on in India, provided cheap transport for the returning GIs and the motorcycle-starved British. Importers and dealers would refurbish the bikes to civilian specification, with a simple paint-job and replacement 16-inch wheels and tyre-hugging mudguards.

During the war years, almost all Harley production was of the WLA model. Altogether some 88,000 bikes were produced. The model proved to be dependable in the vastly differing *conditions of the Europe and North Africa.*

THE END OF THE BEGINNING

The war years claimed millions of lives. Amid the turmoil, the passing of two lives in particular were felt in Milwaukee. Arthur Davidson's brother Walter, who had become the third of the four founding fathers back in 1902, died in February 1942. Walter had been President since 1908.

It was he who had assembled the first Harley-Davidson motorized bicycle which had been designed by Bill Harley and fabricated by Arthur Davidson. In 1903, Walter, a machinist by trade, gave up his job at the railroad to work full-time with his brother and his friend to build motorcycles. It was Walter who proved the dependability of their product, entering endurance competitions with great success on their first production models.

Walter Davidson earned a reputation as a hard-headed – and stubborn – businessman. Many who had personal dealings with him portrayed him as peevish and particularly mean with company money; through shrewd investment of his personal wealth, though, the estate he left stood at almost $5 million. His control of the company's fortunes was similarly successful. He took the company from the famous shed in his

father's back garden to the existing Juneau Avenue works, from a one-bike a week enterprise to a 20,000 bikes a year industry, and the United States' biggest, most successful and most enduring motorcycle manufacturer.

William (Bill) S. Harley did not live to see the end of the war either. He was the third of the four founding fathers of Harley-Davidson to die. He suffered a fatal heart attack in the autumn of 1943, aged 63, sitting on a bar-stool in his favourite club. When we talk of 'Harleys', it's Bill's name we use, as it was Bill Harley and Arthur Davidson who together formed the idea for a motorized bicycle at the turn of the century.

Bill, like Walter Davidson, was a keen motorcyclist right from the early days when he competed to prove the worthiness of his own creations in endurance events around the country. He held a position on the Competition Committee of the American Motorcycle Association (AMA) for 24 years. Towards the end of his life, he began to favour four wheels over two, and withdrew from the business to concentrate on his more artistic hobbies. In his vigorous years he was a dedicated outdoorsman, always a keen angler

The end of World War II brought a brisk trade in refurbished – and repainted – WLAs. Some 15,000 were sold off by the U.S. government, many of them to returning GIs who had fallen in love with Harleys during their wartime service.

and hunter. Indeed his first prototype engine is said to have powered a rowing boat around the local lakes. He had his aesthetic and sensitive side too, spending much time drawing, painting and photographing wildlife.

As Chief Engineer and Designer at Harley-Davidson from the inception of the company until his death, he was the one man responsible for the classic Harley-Davidson engine design. That is not to say he invented the V-twin – far from it. In fact, Bill Harley tended to look to what was already around for his inspiration. However, he dogmatically and usually correctly, built to suit the customer. He had a great empathy for the needs of United States' motorcycling public and met that need in the face of whatever new ideas and trends were going on around him. He sustained the design which endures today, a commercial success, loved by millions, 85 years on.

Post-War Rebels

The post-war era began on a bad note. There occurred an incident, not directly related to the marque, which was to create an undeserved unwholesome image for Harley-Davidson. They have found this image impossible to shake off and have only recently learned to live with it. This particular incident

The FLH Duo-Glide is every Harley collector's dream bike. This example is in the original Calypso red with Birch White tank panels.

marked the first occasion on which the motorcycle was associated with anti-social elements. This association is now an intrinsic part of motorcycling the world over.

An American Motorcycle Association (AMA) clubman's rally took place on July 4, the United States Day of Independence, at

Hollister in California, attended by an impressive 4,000 motorcyclists. Among them were around 500 so-called 'outlaw' motorcyclists who, in a drunken frenzy, ripped up the town – or at least that is how the incident was reported by a sensation-hungry press at the time. A now classic *Life* magazine cover photograph features the atypical drunken slob, lounging on his Harley, (stripped of touring paraphernalia), which stands atop a pile of empty beer bottles. He toasts the camera, a bottle in each hand, his vacant stare reaching far beyond the lens. In the months following, millions would meet his gaze. The upstanding were outraged, the impressionable intrigued.

The disturbance in Hollister was considerable, even though the nature of the crime itself was petty, and required 500 law enforcement officers to bring it under control. The national press had a field day sensationalizing the incident and devoting masses of column space to the bands of Harley-riding outlaws who gave themselves such anti-establishment names as *Satan's Sinners* and *Booze Fighters*.

Duo-Glide Harley-Davidson pannier of double skinned fibreglass.

THE PANHEAD
FLH Duo-Glide of 1959 with overhead valve 74 cu inch V-twin engine. Aluminium cylinder heads and pistons with hydraulic valve lifters. The model came with a 'Victory' camshaft, streamlined mirror-polished intake ports, cadmium plated, closed-end connecting rod bearing retainers and high compression ratio of 9 to 1, producing 60 bhp and massive torque.

There was a choice of four-speed gearbox with head or foot shift; the model shown on these pages has the more popular foot shift. For the Duo-Glide sidecar model, a three-speed gearbox with reverse was available.

The front suspension was called Hydra-Glide by Harley-Davidson. The front forks contained helical springs, damped by oil. The rear suspension was of the swinging arm type with hydraulic shock absorbers, complete with springs enclosed in chrome tubular covers.

Harley advertised the Duo-Glide as having 3-point suspension because the seat post – similar to early Harleys – also had a spring. This gave the saddle spring load for extra comfort.

The Duo-Glide in these photographs has been authentically restored over a three-year period, from a rolling wreck, by Martin Gale of Dorset, England.

It was a worrying and unprecedented phenomenon at the time. This rebellion and 'dropping out' from society was labelled a legacy of the war and an expression of the difficulty many young men experienced when attempting to reintegrate into a placid society after the danger and excitement of battle. There is no doubt that the post-war society in the United States perhaps did not understand or appreciate the deep scars war left on young, fresh minds. War-weary youths were simply expected to return to the same lifestyle which they had led before in their home towns, as though the whole thing had never happened. Certainly the effects of war had been more immediate for Europeans than the majority of non-combatant United States citizens.

Whatever the sociologists and psychologists decided, the fact remained that a new breed of motorcyclist had been born, and sadly for Harley-Davidson it was *their* motorcycle which had been chosen as the epitomizing symbol with which the rebellious youth should demonstrate its

Duo-Glide 120 mph speedometer on gasoline tank.

discontentment with society.

Any sensational incident which captures the United States' public's imagination, especially something emanating from California, inevitably finds its way on to celluloid. In the case of Hollister, it took until 1954 when *The Wild One*, starring Marlon Brando and Lee Marvin, stirred the consciousness of the impressionable and disaffected youth of the United States, with its cast of anti-heroes. The authorities, shocked by what was being portrayed, made matters many times worse by banning the film, and thus elevating it to cult status.

To the lasting detriment of motorcycling in the United States, the bike-riding boozy rednecks of *The Wild One* were glamourized – especially by Marlon Brando, whose part in the film centred on a love interest with a pretty waitress

Above: All original brand-new Harley-Davidson old stock parts were used in this rebuild. The Hydra-Glide forks and brakes assembly were bought, in their original parts boxes, from a local Harley-Davidson dealer.

Below: Duo-Glide with 8-inch diameter front fully enclosed waterproof brake.

(the sheriff's daughter) at the local milk bar. She knew he was trouble, but she couldn't resist him. He was the ideal role model for rebellious youth. Most of the brawling bikers rode stripped Harleys, although 'Johnny' (Brando) rode a Triumph Speed Twin. After all, he wasn't *all* bad.

The film served to entrench several ideas, the most obvious of which was that motorcycle gangs existed in the United States. It showed how they behaved (uncontrollable and anti-social), it showed how they dressed (leather jacket, jeans, boots and jaunty cap), and it showed that if they were *proper* motorcycling rebels, they chose to ride Harley-Davidsons.

All this bad association was beyond the control of Harley-Davidson, who until this film had been doing very well out of Hollywood. Around the time of the

Above: Original Harley handlebar and tank details. Note green light indicator and chrome speedo surround.

Left: Duo-Glide special original seat with cushion-sprung seat post.
Left below: Two accessory spotlights mounted next to the headlight.

Hollister incident, several stars of the era had been raising their profiles still higher by riding around Beverly Hills on Harley-Davidsons. The most notable of these was Clark Gable. Other Harley stars of the time were Keenan Wynn (who publicly condemned the Hollister rowdies), Robert Young, and Robert Taylor. Even Gene Tierney threw a shapely nyloned leg over a 45. Within a few years this glamorous image as the sporting recreational vehicle of the stars would be turned on its head.

This unexpected, unplanned and unwanted image which Harley-Davidson had forced upon them was counter-attacked with a barrage of positive public relations, emphasizing that it was a tiny minority who were spoiling the fun for the majority of sport-loving clubmen. They were ne'er-do-wells who should be ignored, and quite right too! However, the image was there to stay, a constant thorn in the side of the Harley marketing department. Harley-Davidson would continue to ignore the fact that their product had become a symbol of rebellion.

TIDYING UP – A NEW ERA
At the factory, the drawing boards had been put in the cupboard until the end of the war. With the doubt and uncertainty behind them, Harley-Davidson could get on with developing and expanding their range of products. The ten-year-old Knucklehead, now a classic and a

particular favourite of customizers, had some fundamental weaknesses which needed addressing with a fresh approach to top-end mechanics. The very first prototypes of the Knucklehead had led factory tester and engineer Joe Petrali to a showdown with President Walter Davidson over its propensity to throw out oil from its knobbly rocker covers. Ten years into production, the Knucklehead was still doing it. In late 1947 however, the blueprints were realized and two new models were announced for sale in 1948.

Harley-Davidson had kept production at a healthy level throughout the war, averaging around 20,000 bikes a year. The planned production for 1948 was set at 30,000 and happily none would be painted olive green drab. The new models were basically updates of the 61 and 74 heavyweights and the top-end troubles were the first to be eliminated – in theory anyway. Sadly, in practise, it was the same old story with a factory kit following the bikes to the dealers who were to put right problems which the usual all-too-brief testing failed to reveal.

The new models addressed a high-speed/hot weather overheating problem rooted in the cast-iron barrels and heads of the Knucklehead. Now, and forever, heads would be of cast aluminium alloy which dissipate heat better and are not so prone to heat distortion. Oil lines now ran internally.

As with many new ideas built into Harley engines, the hydraulic valve lifter mechanism which featured on the new models, was actually borrowed from the automobile industry, particularly suited as it is, to big slow-revving engines. The idea is that the tappets are self-adjusting and maintain accurate valve clearances, a problem for an engine with such large casts of solid metal whose expansion with heat causes

tolerances to waiver. They made the top-end quieter too. However, like many other Harley 'innovations', they created more problems than they solved and were prone to failure until a long overdue redesign in 1953. Basically, the hydraulic lifter mechanism was placed at the top of the engine, which the oil had a difficult job to reach, making the system too sensitive to oil pressure changes. The remedy was simply to drop them down to just above the cam, thus curing the problem. Hydraulic lifters are still used on the modern 1340 cc *Evolution Harley* engines.

In time-honoured tradition, reaching back to the days of the *Silent Gray Fellow*, the new engine was soon given a nickname by Harley-Davidson fans, which like Knucklehead, sounded more insulting than endearing. The *Panhead* had begun its 17-year production run. It was not difficult to see where the name came from, as the aluminium rocker cover looked just like an inverted saucepan. It was a design aimed at curing the oil-leaks which had been part and parcel of Knucklehead ownership. It was indeed an improvement, but it still leaked oil.

The launch of the new Panhead

at the 1947 conference was no surprise to dealers, but the unveiling of a single-cylinder lightweight two-stroke 125 cc machine at the same meeting was an outright shock. The *Hummer* as it was named, was a new direction for Harley-Davidson, but not one they were to pursue very far. The bike itself did not represent a great investment as the design was part of the spoils of war, taken from the German company DKW. In England, BSA began producing their version, the famous and enduring *Bantam*. For would-be motorcyclists looking for a gentle introduction to the sport in the United States, there was no home-produced alternative to the British lightweight, so the new 125 did find a niche. Indeed, during 1948 Harley-Davidson built over 10,000.

As if to continue the momentum of the Panhead's introduction, the factory finally let go of 40 years of tradition, when hydraulically damped sprung forks were introduced in 1949. Harley also set a precedent with the updated 74, by withdrawing forever the privilege from its customers of naming the new babies. Harley's own marketing department came up with the title, *Hydra-Glide*.

The Silent Gray Fellow began the tradition of calling models with evocative and memorable names, which continues to this day.

Split Personalities

As a new era dawned in the motorcycle history of the United States, another ended with the death of the one surviving founding father of Harley-Davidson. Arthur Davidson and his wife died in a car accident on 30 December, 1950. It was Arthur who had joined Bill Harley in partnership at the turn of the century to create the very first Harley-Davidson motorcycle. He had spent his career, from the earliest days, marketing and selling the bikes and creating a momentum which had carried Harley-Davidson through two wars, the Great Depression and now into the second half of the 20th century where the company's greatest trials lay. Harley-Davidson stewardship now passed fully into the hands of the second generation.

The Hydra-Glide was well received despite its violent break with Harley-Davidson's leading tradition of a link fork. The telescopic forks, enormous as they were, worked well, giving a comfortable ride. The rear end of the bike was considered adequately taken care of by the sprung seat post and a rear tyre which would not be out of place on a car. Comfortable it may have been, but the rigid back end could not be deemed efficient, the rear wheel having trouble staying in constant touch with the road surface.

In 1953, Harley experimented with rear suspension on their Model K 45 Sportster, a 'middle-weight' built to face the British invasion of high-performance machinery. On the track, Norton had beaten Harley three years

Harley Street Racer, built by Mark Shadley of Hanson, Massachusetts, based on the 1977 Harley Sportster. The incredible engraving was done by Dave Perewitz of Cycle Fab. This 'slimstyle' lowrider look is popular at the shows.

running at Daytona; such humiliation on home ground could not be tolerated. In keeping with their usual practice, when faced with foreign technological threats on the racetrack, the AMA moved the goalposts in Harley's favour by banning double overhead cams and therefore the Manx Norton. By 1952, Harley Davidson's new Sportster racer, codenamed the KR, was ready and it was just as well that the rules had changed, as the new bike was in fact, even

slower than the WR, the bike it replaced.

The roadbike featured adoption of some British innovations, such as a hand-controlled clutch and foot-operated gear lever. Rear suspension was by swinging arms and two suspension units to assist traction, and the front was by telescopic fork. In contrast with the modern chassis, the K had an old style sidevalve engine. It did not sell, largely because the public scorned its puny pulling power and in 1955 the engine was bored out to 883 cc (55-inch), ending the run of classic 750 cc (45-inch) capacity. The sidevalve system was not destined to endure. It was a 1921 design trying to work in 1955. In 1957, the engine was given overhead valves like the modern large capacity motors, and re-coded the XL. This motor would be the basis of great international sporting achievement.

The suspension ideas realized in the Sportster were accepted at the factory as the way ahead. In the same year, the XL made its debut, the FL and FLH Hydra-Glide Panheads were given rear suspension along the same lines as the Sportster. The factory named it the *Duo-Glide*. Despite massed shrugging from Harley-Davidson enthusiasts, who considered the rear suspension arrangements unnecessary, the system stayed and remains today (although, in case of the 1988 *Softail,* the units are hidden for the sake of style). As an option, foot gear change and a hand lever clutch were offered, although shunned by the police fleets as they liked to keep their hands free for various tasks of routine law enforcement.

CHOPPING AND CHANGING
It is at this point in the marque's history that the schizophrenic character of the Harley-Davidson emerges. The large-capacity twin had now established itself as the club's standard touring machine. While this respectable group of

Above: Willie G. Davidson's first factory custom - the Super Glide 1200.

Left above: The overhead valve XL motor was first seen in 1957; the heart of this tasteful creation is an XLH engine from 1959. The OHV motor gave greater tuning potential than the sidevalve motor it replaced. This bike is a 74 cu inch capapcity with 70 bhp.

Left: Walter Rasile turned the wreck of a 1959 XLH into a tasteful custom street bike. Lacquered paint in Ice Blue with Dark Blue flames is overpainted in Pearl White.

sportsmen set about dressing their machines for comfort and convenience with boxes, panniers and sidecars, an underlying movement surfaced involving the stripping of machines to the great and lasting dismay of both the clubman and the general public. The chopper was born.

The roots of the chopper's style lie in drag-racing, a sport imported to the United States from Britain, which took off in California in the late 1950s. The typical dragster bike had a lowered chassis, raked-out forks, a rigid rear-end, skinny front wheel, a large rear tyre, no

front brake and a tiny petrol tank. In the interests of saving weight it would be stripped of anything considered not useful in making the bike go faster.

The outlaw biker element watched the transformation of Harley to dragster with interest. Until now, the typical modifications to the outlaw biker's Harley would involve the removal of anything generally considered unnecessary to the basic functioning of the vehicle: crashbars, front mudguard, carriers, windscreen and so on. The rear mudguard would be 'bobbed' –

cut off behind the seat – adding to the 'stripped' look and, in wet weather, giving the more law-abiding citizens following behind something to think about. It also gave the style of machine its name – the *California Bobber*.

As motorcycle drag-racing grew in popularity in the California area, specialist tuning parts manufacturers sprang up making and selling replacement tanks, seats, handlebars and frames to convert bikes to dragster specifications. Low frames with a raked steering-head angle and rigid rear ends were considered the best design for a quick get-away at the strip, giving a more direct drive than the modern machines with rear suspension, and saving more weight. It all made great sense for the sporting-minded bikers who wanted to compete seriously. Such a transformation demanded a generic name for the style of racer and the term 'chopper' was coined and adopted. The name refers to

the practice of cutting and rewelding the frame at the headstock to lower and lengthen the bike, to keep the front wheel down under drop-clutch acceleration.

The outlaw fraternities watched with interest. They soon began to adopt the dragstrip style, buying from the tuning suppliers, chopping their own bikes, fitting lengthened girder forks, tiny front wheels, small tanks and modifying the bikes to suit themselves. The door had been opened and Harley customizing, indeed motorcycle customizing, was established. The Harley was being used as a means of expressing its owner's individuality. The 'chopper' had inspired an entire underground motorcycle movement and had become a permanent feature of motorcycling which would spread throughout the world, to all makes of motorcycle, but with the spirit of the Harley-Davidson big twin at its heart.

The chopper riders could, and still can, be split into two groups: the formalized outlaw clubs and those individuals who simply like the biker style, way of life and the outrageously customized motorcycle. In the United States, the latter style of biker is now an established 'type', and modes of dress and, in its more innocent aspects, behaviour reflect the outlaw clubmember's lifestyle. Long hair, beards, beer-bellies and tattoos are the hallmarks of the Harley-loving biker of the United States. There is no age limit either – indeed they tend to be older individuals who have had some military experience, responsible for a perhaps more cynical outlook and a more boisterous and irreverent attitude towards 'having fun'. The scantily clad 'ol' lady' rides pillion,

Below: This is just the kind of custom special which inspired Willie G. to design the FX1200 Super Glide back in 1971.

Right: Harley riders are serviced by an industry of aftermarket parts suppliers: custom fittings here include Drag Specialities saddlebags, Janner seat and S & S Two Throat carburettor. The amazing murals are by John McCarthy from Hinsdale, New Hampshire.

Below: Panhead Harley-Davidson Duo Glide. On the left is John McCarthy, the biker's builder and painter, and on the right is the owner Bernie Tatro. The bike is called 'The Barbarian'.

Left: 'The Barbarian', paint by Kent Imperial on the 'peanut' gasoline tank. Chrome plating by London Plates, engraving by Del Mar.

Above: Thanks to certain historical incidents and the Mafia-like activities of certain outlaw clubs, bikers have a reputation for lawlessness. For the vast majority, it is undeserved. These individuals broke the speed limit on Daytona Beach.

usually cramped and contorted, knees around her ears, atop a miniscule 'fanny-pad' while the 'ol' man' stretches out comfortably with his feet up on the highway pegs, chin in the breeze. If any lawbreaking goes on among these types, it's generally in connection with 'having fun' and nothing which could be deemed undermining to society.

This lifestyle is in sharp contrast with some of the outlaw clubs, who take their persona more seriously. Their organized crime is alleged to be on a Mafia-like scale in the United States and indeed throughout the world. It is alleged to involve crime such as bike theft, inevitably Harleys in the main, usually executed by third parties – 'wannabe' characters, eager to impress the club members in order to be enrolled. Funds raised this way, it is said, are channelled into more profitable activities like drug dealing. The proceeds from more overt activities, such as music concert promotion and bike show organization are often turned over to charities in a risible demonstration of goodwill and a positive attitude toward society. This is the dark side of biking indeed.

Back in the late 1950s and early 1960s biking was attracting returning Korean War veterans in the way the Second World War had precipitated the outlaw biker movement, but the style now was to be chopper mounted. It was a time, too, of changing attitudes and a shift toward liberalism in the United States, originating in California. There was backlash over the atomic bombing of Japan, over Korea, over McCarthy's paranoia about Communism, added to fears of war with the Soviet Union as the Cold War deepened.

For young men and women this was not a society with a bright future, and 'dropping-out' became a major aspect of the next decade. There were many who sought the simple truths: peace, love and freedom were the catchwords of the day. This attitude was simply not understood by the conservative population and the whole movement was interpreted as 'unAmerican'. The divide between these new ideas of freedom and the conservatism of mainstream society could not have been greater. The concept of freedom of thought and individual expression took hold,

The Harley-Davidson 'Topper' – a 10 cu inch two-stroke single, with fibreglass body. It was launched in the late 1950s and described as 'tops in beauty and tops in performance'.

and for many the ideal vehicle through which to express their individuality and their disaffection with the established 'American Way', was a motorcycle. More than just a symbol of rebellion against the establishment, the motorcycle was viewed as a symbol of freedom. Harley-Davidson shunned this association with vehemence, but given time, would come round. It was, after all, a marketing man's gift on a plate.

Wilfully blind to all this sociology, the folks back in Milwaukee continued their business as usual. Harley-Davidson was doing its level best to ignore the strange mutilations being

wrought on their products and continued to promote their bikes in the time-honoured fashion: as a sporting and healthy outdoor pursuit for the middle classes.

In the late 1950s, Harley-Davidson had the big touring bike and police force market pretty-well sewn up. Indian, their only domestic competitor for so many years had wound up its motorcycle business in the late 1950s. The old United States giant had taken on the European middleweights and had to struggle to compete. The *Indian Chief* was produced in scant numbers after the war, allowing Harley to secure its domination of the market. In 1960, the Harley-Davidson range held nothing between the 165 cc *Teleglide* (the Hummer's successor) and the overhead valve 883 cc (55 cu inch) Sportster XL. The long-serving and trusted sidevalve 45 had been replaced in 1955 by a bored-out

version, the KH, which had proved to be an unpopular sluggard, and its production ceased in 1957. Two versions, a sportster and a tourer, were launched in its place and were instant hits.

Harley-Davidson had the heavyweight market covered, and had also produced some commuter vehicles, such as the *Topper* scooter, the 165 cc *Teleglide* and some odd small runarounds – the *Scat*, the *Pace* and the *Bobcat*, all powered by a new 175 cc two-stroke motor.

The middleweight market, the 250 cc to 500 cc category, was the preserve of the British. There then came about an ostensibly strange but very logical merger with the struggling Italian company, Aermacchi. By buying in 50 per cent of the company, Harley could now fill in its model range gap with cheap bikes from Italy.

Harley adopted a very successful single cylinder 250 cc four-stroke, OHV bike with the cylinder characteristically laid horizontally in line with the frame. It was in fact a Moto Guzzi copy. For the United States market, the bike was renamed the *Sprint* and went on sale in 1961. Despite the bike's 129 kph (80 mph) performance, the United States market turned up its nose; if a motorcycle was not made in the United States and was not a V-twin, it did not constitute a Harley. Apart from this, the United States motorcycle industry was on the verge of its own Japanese invasion.

The Italians of Aermacchi decided to use the new influx of capital to resurrect their racing programme, and had laudable success with 350 cc racers around the circuits of Europe, culminating in Renzo Pasolini's third placing in the 350 cc World Championship of 1966. Arguing that the success was enhancing the marque's sales, the Italians' next step was an overhead cam racer, but Harley pulled the rug – the overhead cam was too expensive. V-twins were, after all, the company's main business.

Harley's Darkest Hour

The Japanese infiltration into the United States' motorcycle market was a shock to the system indeed. Here, suddenly and as though from nowhere, was a new kind of motorcycle. It was oil-tight, clean, neat, high quality, reliable and cheap. Motorcycles had never been 'user-friendly' until these bikes appeared with, worryingly for all, electric starters. The public's

attention was diverted, and Harley-Davidson suddenly stood back and realized it had become complacent. With its erstwhile dominance of the home big bike market, nothing much had happened in the research and development department.

While one section of the biking community was consuming creative Harley-based works of art

from existing stock, the new business for the smaller bore machines was going elsewhere – to Britain and Japan. Although Harley-Davidson did not quite foresee the monster tidal wave heading its way from Japan, the

The Electra Glide. The addition of an electric start and a new name to the Duo Glide created a legend.

factory realized it needed to do something – and quickly. Sales had dropped and profits stood still in the years up to 1965. Harley held a mere six per cent of the home retail market.

The answer was to offer shares in the company for sale to the public, in order to bring in some money to revitalize the flagging marque. After 60 years, the Harley-Davidson marque seemed to be slipping from the families' grasp. In reality, the bulk of the shares were bought by the families, in effect maintaining a dominant control. However, the idea behind the infusion of new capital did not work. Harley's first use of the new capital was to launch a publicity campaign and spruce up the 74 *Duo Glide* by fitting an electric start. Although this created what was undoubtedly the most famous model ever to come out of Milwaukee, it did nothing in the short term. The model was called the *Electra Glide*.

The *Duo's* electric system was uprated to 12 volts from six and for a mere(!) 34 kg (75 lb) weight penalty, new owners could start up at the nudge of a button – but not in the wet. The bike shorted out in these conditions and needed to be redesigned. The overburdened Electra Glide was given more power, but sacrificed smoothness, and it was now overloading its brakes too. A 1965 road test in the United States' magazine *Cycle World,* condemned the front brake as 'laughable'. The factory made up for this in 1972, when they celebrated the 74 cu inch motor's 50th anniversary by making it the first production motorcycle to run hydraulic disc brakes, front and rear. In the short run, however, Harley paid a price for its revised bike. Nevertheless, the Electra Glide would remain the most sought after and dreamed about of new full dresser touring models for the next 25 years – a living legend to this day. Of all motorcycle model names, Electra Glide stands out as the most widely known. Honda's

Full Dress Harley V-twin 1200 Glide of 1972, owned by Richard and Marlene of Naples, Florida.

Goldwing only comes a poor second. Indeed, in 1971 there was even a film named after it: *Electra Glide in Blue*. It starred Robert Blake as a Harley-mounted motorcycle cop with a free spirit. It involved the dream to own a customized all-blue Electra Glide. The two interpretations of the Electra Glide – establishment's law enforcement vehicle and, in another guise, the wheels on which to ride off into the sunset – used the bike as a metaphor for the main character's personal dilemma between conforming and breaking free.

The Electra Glide proved to be a milestone in another respect too, in that the first Electra Glide carried the last Panhead motor. To handle the extra weight, the engine was uprated by use of so-called 'power pac' cylinder heads which increased horsepower by ten per cent. The power came from redesigned combustion chambers, their odd shovel-shape offering the punters yet another opportunity to give the motor its own unofficial

Above: 'Daddy O'. Electra Glide Full Dresser. This is undoubtedly the most famous model ever to come out of Milwaukee. It has been the subject of films, documentaries and the fantasies of millions. The Electra Glide was the last model series to use the Panhead motor and the first to use the Shovelhead. This is a 1200 cc, 66 hp example. It weighs about 300 kg (660 lb) but can still hit 175 kph (108 mph).

name – *Shovelhead*. It was to power the large capacity Harleys throughout the next 15 years.

The Japanese were not the only invaders in Harley's territory. The British marques Triumph, BSA and Norton were uprating their models relentlessly at this time, not in a radical or imaginative way (to their eternal detriment), but always pushing for more power to capture the young enthusiast's attention. The only answer Harley had was the 883 Sportster, in comparison a heavy, unwieldy and sadly slow bike. The British bikes were even encroaching on Harley's fast establishing cult status among the customizers too. Chopped British bikes were increasingly seen as an even further extreme of personal expression.

How Harley had come to find itself in such a mess at a time of post-war economic boom is a question indeed. The answer lies in the fact that Harley-Davidson was and had always been a family business. Those who ran the business were in their positions because of their name, not their commercial ability. Those who would rise to high office on the strength of their abilities were always kept out of the key executive posts by Harleys and Davidsons. They were men with fixed ideas about what they wanted to build rather than what the customers wanted. It is one reason why a design of engine, which is basically limited in its development

company into the modern era. The post-war executives, faced with serious decisions, stuck to the traditional family policies.

A consequence of this was that the Juneau Avenue factory was hopelessly outdated and incapable of meeting the burgeoning post-war demand, ten times that of the pre-war level. There had been no serious investment in new models; Harley were and are still famous for their slow turnover in model

By 1967 the Harley board was desperate. They had tried everything seemingly possible and it had not proved to be enough. The problem was too fundamental. With the company on the brink of ruin, a decision was reached. The only answer was to look for a large conglomerate to buy out Harley-Davidson – in reality, liquidation was not far off and the potential ramifications for the families who

potential by its 45° V-twin configuration, exists today.

Still, with little competition, this way of conducting business worked adequately until the founding fathers died, and power was disseminated among the succeeding relatives. Decision-making, once a matter of calling together a handful of men who had been running the company since the days of the back garden shed, became a murky affair. There was no authority, no one to take the

Cruising the beach at Daytona on a 'Shovelhead'.

specification. *Cycle World* put it well in the mid 1960s, reasoning that they rarely tested Harleys as they changed in specification about as regularly as Volkswagens! More seriously, a whole sector of the market – the middleweights – was ignored, to be filled by the British and later the Japanese, with their revolutionary production techniques.

had just sunk so much of their own personal wealth into the company, were frightening.

Harley-Davidson had two takers; one prospect was attractive, the AMF (American Machine and Foundry Company), the other, Bangor Punta, was not, although both had good intentions. The favoured group, the AMF, a manufacturer of industrial machinery that was primarily leisure-orientated, won the day after much bitter legal wrangling.

This worked well for the existing shareholders, whose stock rose in value as the two prospective buyers tried to outbid each other. Indeed shares bought for $6 just a couple of years or so before, were now quoted at $42 at the time of takeover. Harley-Davidson was sold for $21 million. It had been the right action for them at least.

Harley-Davidson was taken over by the AMF in January 1969, and although ultimate control was

within the latest generation of bikers, a fact which the management had chosen to ignore in their disapproval of such types. The Harley chopper custom spares market was mushrooming – another area of potential commercial success, which was deliberately ignored by the company. The management clung to the old image of motorcycle clubmen, who rode the touring dressers and were mature,

building their own custom bikes to satisfy such customer demand at a time when standard factory bikes were falling in popularity.

The most famous biker/road film ever made hit the cinemas of the United States and the world in 1969. It was called *Easy Rider*, and starred Peter Fonda, Dennis Hopper and Jack Nicholson. For a film which cost $375,000 to make, it was phenomenally successful, making Columbia Pictures $20

finally wrested from the founding families, the managerial hierarchy stayed in place, with its cadres of Harleys and Davidsons throughout. However, once the decrepit state of the company came to light, a thorough investigation was made, indicting the family management's apparent incompetence and blinkered, high-handed attitudes.

Meanwhile, the profile of Harley-Davidson had never been so high. It had attained cult status

Harley-Davidson Sporster of 1962, a model that was sluggish and no match for British competition of its era. Mark Shadley and Mike Esterbrooks from Rockland, Massachusetts, exchanged the 883 cc engine for a 1340 cc one!

traditional and conservative. That this type of motorcyclist was becoming a rare breed in proportion to the new 'biker' seemed not to be the issue with the executive. Even dealers were

million richer. It was *The Wild One* all over again for Harley-Davidson, entrenching in the world's mind that choppers were Harleys and Harleys were choppers, and that these motorcycles symbolized freedom and rebellion, for good and for bad. It projected into the minds of the public at large the image of the bikers – no longer a strange hippy fringe movement of weird motorcyclists, kicking around California. The film explained the symbolism of the customized bike, the freedom of expression and the freedom to take off, regardless of society's opinions. If it were up to the old guard at Harley-Davidson, the film would have been banned. To them, this was not how Harleys should be portrayed.

The AMF had no prejudices or preconceptions about how they should be catering for their customers. Significantly the AMF's first bold advertising campaign appealed directly to the new generation of Harley fanatics, calling the bike the 'All-American Freedom Machine'. At the same time, the AMF expanded production and the model range, by utilizing a plant located at York, Pennsylvania, where all Harley-Davidson machines are assembled today. Engine manufacture continues at the Milwaukee factory.

At this time, a new figure began to make his presence felt in the management hierarchy in a way which would have had many a late Harley or Davidson turning in his grave. William G. Davidson, son of

William H. Davidson and grandson of William A. Davidson the co-founder, had joined the company in 1963, and was working in the design and styling department, eventually becoming its head. As such, he would rise to the status of the most influential person in the company in terms of the Harley-Davidson image, and everything it stands for today. Willie G., as he styles himself, was responsible for the first Harley-Davidson factory custom – the FX1200 *Super Glide* – the first large capacity Harley to appear minus any of the usual touring paraphernalia. Nor did it have any sporting pretensions as a fast, relatively lightweight machine. Launched in 1971, it amounted to nothing less than a 1950s chopper! It was style for style's sake and gave more than a hint of where Harley's future

Daytona Promenade – Pink Rosebud chopper, with English SU carb and chrome mesh air cleaner.

prosperity, or rather, hope for survival lay. The tank and seat unit were painted patriotic red, white and blue, a colour scheme named by the factory *Sparkling America*.

Amid all this glory, complaints were flooding in from dealers that the latest machines off the speeded-up production line were showing faults and that quality control was obviously failing. Although steps were taken to tighten up procedures, it was enough for dealers and the enthusiasts to carp about a drop in standards under AMF ownership. Would Harley ever be the same again? Further discontent was fostered by the factory's almost unbelievable policy of putting the onus for final quality inspection on the dealers, thus giving the factory an escape from warranty claims. The quality control problems were often beyond the ability of dealers to detect or rectify, however, and owners subsequently suffered. It was not long before the sarcastic slogan 'Buy a Harley, buy the best – ride a mile and walk the rest!'

Left: The film Easy Rider *fired the imagination of free-thinking bikers the world over. Overnight, the long-forked chopper changed from being a symbol of rebellion and lawlessness to a symbol of freedom and individualism. This radical Shovelhead sensibly dispenses with a front brake.*

Above and left: California Dreamin' – in Florida. For East-coasters, Daytona Beach is the only place to show off your chopper. This example is a Shovelhead – note the gold-plated pushrod tubes. The forks' suspension relies on their flexibility. The bike has a rigid rear end, but the rider spares himself permanent injury by using a spring saddle.

Left: Baby Harley. Herb Martin and his daughter Michelle marvel at a miniature exhibit at Daytona's Rat's Hole custom show. It is a 1950s Panhead with a 150 cc home-made engine. It took six years to build.

gained currency, to Harley-Davidson's lasting detriment.

A large part of the problem stemmed from the very nature of the company the AMF had taken on, staffed as it was by so many lifelong employees, who virtually hand-assembled bikes and finished key parts on the assembly line in their own time-honoured manner. When the AMF started gearing up the whole operation, splitting manufacture and assembly between

Milwaukee and York, it was no wonder these particular procedures were missed. Under the AMF, the same parts were making a different whole. The situation reached an intolerable pitch for the factory when the Harley-Davidson Owners' Association's newsletter, *Gear Box,* started running technical features on how to put right mistakes made in production.

The AMF had paid a sizeable sum for Harley-Davidson, following it up with millions in investment, but it was investing in outdated techniques and trying to sell outdated ideas. Harley-Davidson's range at this time consisted of the 1200 cc Electra Glide, two versions of the Super Glide 1200, two 1000 cc Sportsters, and six lightweights. This was the time when bikes like the highly sophisticated (and desirable) Honda Goldwing were actually being assembled in the United States. Kawasaki were hitting the market with their high-powered, bulletproof-engined Z-series of 900 cc and 1000 cc fours. The police contracts were lost and Harley-Davidson's only remaining preserve – the big tourer market – had begun to be served much more efficiently and cheaply by the Japanese, who were not bound by old traditions. Their brief was to capture the interest of motorcyclists and non-motorcyclists in any way they could. By the mid-1970s, the AMF was beginning to tire of its new acquisition. Harley-Davidson was open to offers.

Top: A 1974 XL, from the moody AMF era, customized by Dan O'Connell of Stamford, Connecticut. Purists would say that the only decent thing to do to a Harley of the mid-1970s is to strip it and rebuild it to your own liking. This one has a C & J Custom frame. The fancy carburettor is a Weber.

Opposite: A 93 cu inch custom – a beauty built by Mallard Teal of White Bear Lake, Minnesota. He runs Motorworks, a Harley shop where he rebuilds engines and transmissions. This SBF-framed Harley was built from spare parts, and is a show winner.

Overleaf: Harley-Davidson XLCR Cafe Racer. Originally 1000 cc and in black, with twin rear shock absorbers, this is a customized example of Willie G. Davidson's second styling experiment'– it bombed. The bike had the sporty look but would not deliver the goods. Ironically, like many Harley flops, it became a collector's item.

Above: Note Police Special Speedo on the tank top.

Above: Candy Brandywine with Flames for the tank.

Above: Vented drive chain cover, all chrome.

1980 to the Present Day

AMF, Harley-Davidson's owners, realized too late that the booming motorcycle market of the 1960s and 1970s held little demand for the kind of traditional, outdated and sadly, unreliable machinery which they were spending so much money promoting. When they bought into the company in 1971, it was not so much a going concern, as going under, and the expected revitalization of Harley-Davidson needed a much more fundamental overhaul.

In the period 1970-1980, the Japanese ruled the motorcycle world, replacing, updating and completely revising models year after year. The bikes were high performance, high quality and altogether reliable. Harley's answer was to continue with the FLH Electra Glide, producing two models, one with a 1200 cc (74 cu inch) engine, and a limited run 1340 cc (80 cu inch) model. As well, there were two versions of the *Super Glide*, the 750 cc (45 cu inch) flat-tracker XR750 and Willie G.'s 1978 creation, a compact, all-black 1000 cc (60 cu inch) 'cafe racer' called the XLCR. It was hardly a bold defence against the Eastern onslaught.

This Cafe Racer was built by Donnie Smith. The tasteful yellow paint was by Kevin Winter, striping by Dave Bell, and engraving by Eagle Motorcycle engraving.

Willie G.'s black XLCR was an attempt to capitalize on the street-racer customizing fashion. Road racer rolling chassis kits proliferated, aimed at putting the superbly powerful Japanese engines into frames which could handle the horsepower. Japanese chassis technology was sadly overshadowed by its motor engineering prowess. These canyon-racer kit specialists were typified by the Rickman Brothers of England and Bimota of Italy, who built chassis with strong frames, top quality suspension and brakes and fitted four-cylinder motors of Suzuki, Kawasaki and Honda. Willie G.'s Harley version had the looks, but unfortunately not the performance of these specials. As such it was not at all popular. Ironically the machine is a collectors' item today, barely 15 years on.

In 1980 a new 'King of the Highway' was introduced, a monster 1340 cc (80 cu inch) tourer which even out-dressed the Electra Glide. It was designated the FLT, or *Tour Glide*. It had a redesigned frame and light, quick steering which made manoeuvring the bulky 360 kg (800 lb) giant surprisingly effortless. Up until now, all models had been four-speed; the FLT with a fifth overdrive ratio could lope along the highway at 96 kph (60 mph) with the engine turning at less than 3000 rpm.

Another model of note, which would set a trend for the future, was the *Sturgis*, a 1340 cc (80 cu inch) all-black Low Rider fitted with a so-called 'new' system of final drive – a belt. In truth, belt drives had been used on Harleys 60 years beforehand, but this new system used modern technology. The toothed belt, made of *Kevlar*, was hailed as the ideal compromise between shaft drive and chain, in that it was light, made for a smooth transmission and would give up to 65,000 km (40,000 miles) service without requiring lubrication or

adjustment. It was a good idea, perfectly suited to the Harley's modest horsepower but large torque; it was to be a feature of all 1340 cc (80 cu inch) bikes produced after 1985, and in 1991 would be used on the *Sportster* range. In the short run, though, the belt was prone to failure and the belt drive was swapped back to chain. This turned out to be a problem which could be overcome (and indeed many aftermarket suppliers at the time offered perfectly reliable replacements).

In 1981, AMF were more than ready to see Harley-Davidson pass from their control. It would be an easy transition back into 'private' hands as the new owners were already running the company; it was a management buy-out. The deal was masterminded by Vaughn Beals, an AMF executive who had been in charge of Harley-Davidson operations. He secured funds amounting to $80 million from a consortium of four banks, led by Citicorp Bank.

At a Daytona press conference Beals was quoted as saying: 'From 1969 through 1980, AMF's substantial capital investment in the motorcycle and golf car businesses permitted Harley-Davidson revenues to grow from $49 million to approximately $300 million.' This statement, although paying great tribute to AMF's commitment to the motorcycle factory, was a nice way of saying AMF had been pouring millions into a bottomless pit and is, in fact, the real reason Harley-Davidson still exists today. Harley-Davidson, of which AMF took control 11 years earlier, was a spent force and, throughout the 1970s remained an anachronism.

AMF was Harley's life support system for this decade. In England, companies like Triumph and Norton were in exactly the same position as Harley-Davidson, producing machines which had been designed some 40 years before with no ammunition to fight the

Japanese invasion. Those famous British marques died their natural deaths, irretrievably out-moded and under-developed, victims of their own inadequate management. Their names are still revered, and indeed have been revived in 1990, attached to modern machinery, but in an almost cynical capitalization on the nostalgia and goodwill still felt by enthusiasts.

ALL IN THE FAMILY
Harley-Davidson would certainly have died in 1970 without the financial injections from AMF, a company which had never understood exactly what it was taking on – a range of obsolete models with a tiny market of die-hard touring-orientated enthusiasts. Meanwhile, throughout the 1970s, the cult of the Harley-Davidson name grew, and with it a yearning for machines of the old style. A reactionary movement was brewing, a kick-back against Japanese fine-art engineering and what some saw as clockwork, bland motorcycles. The company was bought out and the new owners of the Harley-Davidson factory stood to cash in on all this latent goodwill. All they had to do was play their cards right, without being overshadowed by a huge bureaucracy.

This new state of affairs was destined to be a true rebirth of the marque. The new board wanted to sever all ties with AMF and the bad image the association had created for Harley. Beals was sure that the company could be run far more effectively as an independent concern, determining its own direction, not as part of a constraining group strategy, as had been the case with AMF. He and the new board sought to reassure dealers and inspire the public from the outset. The emphasis of the publicity campaign accompanying the buy-out was that the ownership was passing back into 'family' hands, a return to the good old days of Harley-Davidson.

Although not strictly true – of the individuals who formed the new board only Willie G. Davidson could claim to be 'family' – it was never doubted that motorcycle enthusiasts were now in charge. The family concept was almost symbolic, intended to embrace all the dealers and enthusiasts who were Harley-Davidson's long-lost and neglected children.

To publicize the passing of ownership back into private hands, the new shareholders rode together from York, Pennsylvania, to Milwaukee, Wisconsin, under the banner – *The Eagle Soars Alone*. It was a particularly appropriate publicity stunt, symbolizing Harley's return home. The board sought to make Harley-Davidson a success not primarily for commercial reasons, but because of their belief in the product and to revitalize the vast amount of goodwill the name had accrued over its long history, not just in the United States, but world-wide. Here was a gamble which would pay off.

The new management's first step was to introduce new production methods at York, until then only practised in Japan. Called MAN (materials as needed) or 'just-in-time' production, the idea was to do away with large stocks of parts awaiting assembly and build bikes according to orders from dealers. Stocks of parts and finished bikes just represented tied-up capital. Rather than having a production run of one model at a time, the new system allowed all models to be mixed on the production line at one time, with the specific parts for each bike awaiting assembly behind the production-line worker.

It was an efficient use of capital and no worker's time was ever wasted: every time a worker touched a part it was to add value to it: from finishing to painting to final assembly. Quality control procedures took precedence over any production goals, and the line workers themselves were encouraged to express their views

about ways of improving quality, in contrast to the old way of simply carrying out orders handed down from on high. The net effect was to instil great pride among the workers. The programme was soon expanded, taking in the Milwaukee engine and gearbox factory and reaching right to dealership level under the slogan *I Make The Eagle Fly*.

In 1981, the new Harley-Davidson faced the biggest threat to its existence yet – the dumping of over a million foreign bikes on to the United States' market. It was a time of economic recession and high interest rates, and Harley-Davidson cut back production and laid off workers in the face of a huge fall in demand for big bikes, but Japan continued to produce at record levels. With big-bore Japanese bikes being offered for sale at half the price of the Harleys, no matter how the product was improved, it could not possibly look competitive alongside such cheap and high-quality bikes.

By 1982, Harley-Davidson was producing bikes at half its potential capacity. Company Chairman Vaughn Beals went to the government for assistance. In response, President Reagan placed a tariff on all imported bikes over 700 cc, to last five years, declining year by year at the rates of 45 per cent, 35 per cent, 20 per cent, 15 per cent and 10 per cent. If it had not been for Harley's modernization campaign, which had begun when the company was under AMF control, it is doubtful the International Trade Commission would have entertained the request.

In 1982 a new era also began in Harley-Davidson's public relations methods, with the establishment of a factory-sponsored owners' group, the Harley Owners' Group or HOG. The club would organize rallies (national and international), local runs, shows and charity events. The Muscular Dystrophy Association was, and still is, given HOG's full support.

It was another step in the new Harley-Davidson's capitalization on their great history and the goodwill and, indeed, patriotism felt for the all-American marque. Everyone who was touched by Harley-Davidson was to be made to feel a part of a great family. People would ride Harley-Davidson as a way of life, rather than as a weekend hobby; Harley was being presented as an alternative to what the Japanese had defined as motorcycling. They were not only trying hard to win customers, they aimed to keep them.

Furthermore, right from the start of the new era of ownership, the company clamped down on any other company using Harley logos, names or symbols associated with Harley-Davidson. They would issue licences to those who wanted to use the company's logos, but for a fee. Anyone who continued making such associations would be issued with legal notices to 'cease and desist'. From now on, no one would make money out of Harley-Davidson's glorious name but Harley-Davidson. It was a move which made sound commercial sense for a company trying to re-establish itself as a name to trust. At the same time, it hurt many businesses who had kept faith in the company through the hard times and sustained the cult of Harley-Davidson to the point where it could capitalize on that cult itself for its own commercial good.

In another unprecedented marketing ploy in 1985, Harley showed how serious they were about keeping their new customers; they began contending with a customer's urge to trade in a first Harley for a Japanese bike. Harley-Davidson began subsidizing an offer to give a customer the original sale value of a Sportster as the trade-in value for a larger capacity Harley. Indeed then, and today, the Sportser was seen by Harley-Davidson as a loss-leader, priced more than competitively against Japanese offerings, to entice bikers

and new customers into the world of Harley riding. Today in the United Kingdom, there is a £2,500 price differential between the 883 and the cheapest 1340 cc (80 cu inch) bike.

By 1985, however, Harley-Davidson had the confidence in their products to attract as much attention to its bikes as it could. The previous year had seen the introduction of the Evolution engine, a watershed in Harley history. Rumours abounded that Harley, under AMF, had consulted with the Japanese and the Germans over the prospect of completely revising their engines. In fact, the project, begun in 1977, had been conducted entirely on United States' soil.

THE EVOLUTION REVOLUTION

Before 1980, the ground-rules had been made by the Japanese that a motorcycle should be totally reliable. Governments around the world, including that of the United

The awesome XR1000, based on the successful XR750 race motor. The bike was introduced in 1984, but did not impress the public. Its considerable tuning potential was realized too late for commerical success.

States, were setting new, improved standards in terms of clean-running engines. Every year the standards were tightened as the concern over pollution became an environmental – and political – top priority. Noise and exhaust emissions were prime targets. For all these reasons, the Harley engine of old just would not do. This time, however, Harley-Davidson were ready!

The Evolution engine, as the revised motor was called, was announced in 1983 and would carry Harley at least a decade on and most probably into the 21st century. Naturally, it was still a low-tech air-cooled 45 degree

V-twin with push-rod operated overhead valves, as had been its Shovelhead predecessor. The 1340 cc (80 cu inch) motor (unlike the 'unit construction' Sportster) still had a separate gearbox. Harley's marketing strategy and the desires of its target customer dictated that the engine could be of no other configuration.

The main differences were to the top-end; the crankcases remained the same. The alloy cylinders used shrunk-in iron liners and, it was claimed, gave a 75 per cent better heat dissipation. Flat-top Mahle-type pistons replaced the domed pistons of the Shovelhead, and the valves were re-angled for improved combustion (although a steeper intake angle would have been preferable for a better down-draft). The new engine could not afford to weep oil, and indeed, has proved oil tight. The cylinder head studs now ran right through the head and barrel to keep it so. The old contact-breaker ignition was

55

discarded in favour of breakerless computerized electronic ignition. Starting would never be a problem again. The new motor was 15 per cent more powerful, more fuel efficient and totally reliable.

Even so, the motor had a modest, even embarrassing, power output for such a big displacement engine, in comparison to Japanese bikes of the time. However torque was high, and the motor gave adequate performance for what were, after all, highway and street cruisers. In any case, they fulfilled all requirements of the Harley marketing department. The Evolution motor would be the foundation for Harley's stunning turnaround and success.

The engine was introduced on five models in 1985 after a wholly successful and much lauded debut in the all-new FXRS *Sport-Glide* of the previous year. All 'Evo' engines of 1340 cc (80 cu inches), would be rubber-mounted and have *Kevlar* belt final drive. Sportsters, also receiving the 'Evo' treatment in 1985, remained solidly mounted with chain drive for the time being. Initially the Sportster appeared as a solidly mounted 883 cc (55 cu inch) engine at a very competitive price; in the United States $800 less than the XLH1000 pre-Evo model, which was still in the model line-up, although for not much longer. A 1200 cc (74 cu inch) bored-out version of the 883 was to supersede it, and close the door forever on the Shovelhead and Harley's oil-stained past.

This was not before an attempt was made to satiate performance freaks with the introduction in 1984 of the XR1000, however, by Harley's standards a stripped high-performance bike, based on the XR750 flat-tracker. With Harley-supplied aftermarket tuning parts designed by Harley-employee Jerry Branch, the bike was a flyer even by Japanese standards. It was the most powerful streetbike the factory

has ever produced, but was a showroom flop due to lack of publicity over the availability of the Branch hop-up parts. Ironically, it is now much sought after by collectors.

In 1984, after being shunned for so long by reason of unreliability and uncompetitive performance and price, Harley won back the support of the California Highway Patrol. Although the factory is alleged to have subsidized each bike of a 155 units order by $385 each to undercut Kawasaki, it was at least recognition that Harley was once more producing machines suitable for police usage.

Chief Executive of Harley Davidson, Rich Teerlink, at Daytona '91 – helping out with the Poker Run.

PUBLIC IMAGE UNLIMITED
In 1986 amid this renaissance of the Harley marque, the main investor in the company, Citicorp Bank, asked for its money back. With the new confidence in the company and its patently bright future, there was no problem in raising the necessary cash by again going 'public' with a share offer. The operation was masterminded by Rich Teerlink, then Chief Financial Officer, who would later become President and Chief Executive of the company. The cash from the share sale was sufficient to pay off Citicorp and enable Teerlink

to broaden the company's earnings base with a takeover of Holiday Rambler Corp, a major manufacturer of up-market motorhomes. Harley-Davidson was going from strength to strength.

Although Vaughn Beals can take a good deal of credit for the stunning turnaround in fortune of the company, the contribution of Willie G. Davidson, head of the styling department, had profound effects on the fortunes and change of direction the company would undergo.

Willie G. had long recognized Harley-Davidson's potential to capitalize on the attractive rebel biker image with which the marque had been so long associated. Unlike the generation before him, Willie G. accepted and embraced those who had adopted Harley as a cult symbol for freedom and personal expression, and during the AMF period, he actively associated with all lovers of Harley-Davidson. Dressing in the biker/outlaw style so reviled by his forebears, Willie G. hit the road in *Easy Rider* style, and for the first time in the factory's long history, asked the people what they wanted from Harley-Davidson.

The end results of such a grass roots survey can be seen throughout the whole Harley range today. Fundamentally it was identified that no one wanted Japanese-like progress; it was nostalgia for classic old models which excited fans and inspired customizers. This was reflected in Willie G.'s designs for new models, the best example of which is the *Softail*. This is a modern replica of the Hydra Glide, the first Harley to feature telescopic forks. More importantly, the bike had the appearance of a hard-tail, that is, no rear suspension. In fact it did have two rear suspension units, cleverly hidden and laid horizontally, in-line, under the machine. To the casual observer, the bike is indistinguishable from a restored bike of the 1950s. Although the unconventional suspension arrangements preclude the use of rubber mounts, the bike has proved a huge success.

The concept was taken an outrageous step further, in the *Springer Softail*, launched in 1988 to mark the 85th anniversary of the marque. The Springer had girder forks which went out in 1948 in favour of telescopic forks, but in a style never actually seen on a factory bike before; the massive chrome girders and skinny front wheel had been the erstwhile preserve of custom shops, such as *Jammer* and *Custom Chrome*, who had been offering such conversions for years.

CUSTOMIZING CUSTOM
In 1991, the Harley range consisted of an 883cc (55 cu inch) Sportster with a belt-drive and five-speed option, a 1200 cc (74 cu inch) Sportster (both with factory custom variants); the 1340 cc (80 cu inch) FXRS Super Glide (with custom variants); the FXRT tourer complete with panniers and fairing fitted with a superb stereo; the 1340 cc (80 cu inch) *Heritage Softail* (with custom variants: the *Softail Custom*, the *Springer Softail* and the *Fat Boy* – a Softail with solid wheels and chunky styling); the Electra Glide (with two full dresser variants); and the FLT *Tour Glide*.

A new model launched in 1990, the FXDB *Sturgis*, launched another new line of design for Harley-Davidson, contained in the Dyna Glide chassis. This was the response to poor sales of the FXR series which was shunned by the traditionalist Harley fans because of its triangulated frame design around the battery box. It looked too 'Japanese'. The new chassis was 'internal', which basically replaced the triangulated part with a single post hidden by the battery box and the electrics panel. The design also tidied up the wiring loom and moved the oil tank from behind the rear cylinder to under the engine.

The new frame was also stronger, being cast and forged rather than stamped and welded as before.

The Sturgis, a limited edition of 1700, was followed the year after by another limited run, called the *Daytona*, which also featured the Dyna Glide chassis, launched at Daytona in 1991. This bike was basically the same as the Sturgis but with twin discs. The Dyna Glide chassis would ultimately replace the FXR series.

Launching limited-edition runs is part of a firm policy with the new Harley-Davidson Company which, in sensible recognition of its past, is very wary of overproduction and

Willie G.Davidson, Head of Design at Harley-Davidson.

being left high and dry with surplus stocks should demand fall for their bikes. The term 'Limited Edition' virtually guarantees the model will sell out, and has been used with three models launched in the first years of the new decade – the Sturgis, the Fat Boy and the Daytona.

This policy of building strictly to advance orders rather than perceived or anticipated demand, covers all models. The factory sets its own production levels, based on conservative interpretations of dealer orders from each country. Indeed, dealer orders are often slashed as much as 60 per cent by the factory for certain models.

It is a controversial policy, but

from Harley-Davidson's point of view, is merely prudent. The result is a constantly lean market, with demand always outstripping supply. These austere measures, although frustrating for those who do not order in advance, has created, in some markets at least, a situation where manufacturers' recommended retail prices need never be dropped to secure sales. Price wars, common among dealers in any other marque, are unheard of. Harley prices are non-negotiable and dealers are kept happy. Furthermore, Harley-Davidson will never be exposed to the vagaries of fashion and trends.

The bubble of popularity cannot burst as it is never allowed to grow.

Life is not entirely negative for the customer, however. The policy works in his favour, too, by creating a healthy secondhand market for Harleys. In the United Kingdom in 1991, a two-year-old Sportster will sell for only about £200 less than its original price. Compared to other marques, a Harley-Davidson's classic qualities and saleability make it a sound investment.

Overleaf: Inspiration for a factory custom bike snapped at the Rock Store, Santa Monica. The Heritage Softail of 1987 is Harley's response to those who like the hardtail look from pre-Duo Glide days, but do not have the time to build their own.

Strange Customs –
The Harley-Davidson Specials

Anyone who counts himself or herself a Harley-Davidson afficionado must one day make a pilgrimage to one of the great Harley-Davidson rallies. Daytona and Sturgis are the two main gathering places where Harley riders from every American state and every country arrive in their thousands – over 100,000 in the case of Sturgis – just to meet one another.

It is at these rallies where every

facet of the cult of Harley-Davidson can be witnessed. Daytona Beach in Florida is the venue for what was originally just an annual race meeting at the famous Daytona Speedway, but down on the main drag, it is a different story. Thousands of Harley fans arrive with their bikes in the first week in March. They

Harleys at the Rock Store in the Santa Monica mountains.

arrive in trucks, by plane, and some even ride there, just to be part of what has become a Harley rally. The racing, for these folk, is secondary, if not forgotten. There is a strange split in the 'types' who visit Daytona: those who are there for the racing – the Daytona 200-miler is the highlight of the week and is a four-way tussle among the big manufacturers – and those who are there to be part of Bike Week on Daytona Beach.

The Harley-Davidson Company moves its whole management and executive to Daytona for Bike Week. The HOG organization is monumental, with over 20 events happening during every day of the whole week to keep the bikers amused. Everything from Pig Races to Poker Runs and bike shows. This large number of events takes no account of other entertainments such as the Rat's Hole show. At *Daytona '91*, Harley-Davidson's President and Chief Executive, Rich Teerlink, was meeting the folks at a Poker Run. Teerlink was manning the desk, handing out the clues and cards to those taking part. He had time for everyone and showed a genuine enjoyment in meeting and befriending the people for whom his company builds bikes. A top executive was at each station of the Poker Run, doing exactly the same! The week ends with a five-mile procession from the beach to 'Harley Heaven', an enclosure on the infield of the speedway, for Harley owners only. This spectacular parade takes the best part of an hour to pass by with every conceivable – and inconceivable – special on display.

To enable onlookers to appreciate the variety show at a more leisurely pace, many of the bikes seen around Daytona Beach

Above: Daytona is not just for hairy Harley brutes and their 'mommas' – sometimes grandma shows up too! Dot on her pink dresser is a Daytona regular.

Right: The Boot Hill Saloon, Main Street, is the favourite haunt of Harley biker folk during their annual pilgrimage to Daytona. Most come just to 'hang out' rather than to watch the races.

Overleaf: Harley Shovelhead outside the Boot Hill Saloon during Daytona Speed Week.

are often on display parked up in Main Street, their proud owners lurking not too far way, usually keen to answer any questions an interested passer-by may have. The cream of United States customizing can be pored over at one of the most famous Harley custom shows held anywhere: The *Rat's Hole*. This was held in the Ocean Civic Center car-park in 1991. The perimeter fence was covered in black plastic bin liners to encourage people to come inside and look around, rather than simply 'rubber-neck' over the top.

The show did not cater exclusively to Harleys, but it was clear which make of machine the customizers favoured. It is as though they are paying some sort of homage to the marque, as though they revere it as a symbol of individualism, self-expression and – a feeling that is never too far away from the United States consciousness – patriotism.

Above: The Rat's Hole – the best and largest custom bike show in the world. The photograph shows a judge wearing the official T-shirt, looking at a Full Dress Harley.

Above and right: A Full Dress Harley Fourteen Hundred little lamps.

ART ON WHEELS
Talking to the creators of these works of art – and many of these bikes cannot be described as anything less than this – often reveals them to be the result of years of effort, untold hours of thought and work and careful execution. One individual took six years to complete his project. It was a perfect, working, scale model of a Panhead hardtail chopper appropriately sized for a three year-old child. The only question he couldn't answer about his project was 'Why?'. This is a question difficult for many Harley fans to answer, not because they have not thought about it, but it seems to be difficult for some individuals to express their feelings about what the marque represents for them. Tattoos often say more than words!

Right above: Custom Chopper Harley Shovelhead, winner at Rat's Hole.

Left: Trooper Trudeau's four-wheeler Harley – a 1941 V-Twin sitting inside a Harley sidecar body of 1936, is registered as a motorcycle in Florida. Trooper's company, Southern Custom, built and designed the tubular frame to make this 45 cu inch flathead into a 160 kph (100 mph) kart.

Below: Custom Gold Plated.

Bottom: Winner of the Trike competition – a ground-upwards three wheeled invention named 'Bear Catcher'. Harley-Davidson built their own commercial three-wheeler vehicle powered by the 45 sidevalve motor – the Servi-Car – between 1932 and 1974.

The cult of the customized Harley grew up in California, and is still part of the scene there. Fine weather is the best catalyst for motorcycle development and mixed with a free and easy way of life, the Harley customizing business has been allowed to grow into an industry there. It has been possible since the early 1960s to build a complete Harley-Davidson 'clone' without using one part made in Milwaukee – or any part of the United States for that matter. Many aftermarket parts are made in Far Eastern countries where labour is cheap. Many individuals have achieved international fame as custom Harley builders, the most notable being Arlen Ness.

Custom Chrome is a well-known 'chop-house', or customizing workshop, based in Morgan Hill, California. They boast the world's finest products for Harley-Davidson, a claim with which certain parties in Milwaukee might well take issue. Custom Chrome publishes a 500-page illustrated catalogue containing over 6000 non- standard parts which can be fitted to Harleys. Many have been designed by John Read, alias 'Uncle Bunt', Britain's most famous customizer of the 1970s and early 1980s. He now works for Custom Chrome as a designer, lured to California by the magical combination of sunshine and dollars.

Left: Chrome, Gold Plate and Flames.

Left and above: Snakes, ladies and tigers are popular on Harley custom tanks.

Left: Pretty round Harley tank, with angled Weber carburettor.

Right and below: Coffin-style tank – 'The Gray Remnant'. Historic painting, chrome Skinners' Union carburettor from England, and trick exhaust.

Above: 1970 Harley-Davidson Sportster street racer style. Chrome and gold plating by South Shore, and engraving and paint by Cycle Fabrication. Note the S and S carburettor with air ram. Owner, Ed Kerr from Carlisle, Pennsylvania, did all the detailing on this street racer 'lowrider'. The amazing depth of detail has produced a winner at all the shows.

THE BIG TURNAROUND

Officially, Harley-Davidson cocked a disdainful snook at the customizing business as it took off in California in the 1960s. The movement was so big, however, it could not be ignored and certainly was not about to go away. The company realized as it passed through AMF ownership that a vast, multi-million dollar market based entirely on their name, reputation, and products, was booming behind their backs. Under AMF, the board took a decision to clamp down hard on anyone who was using the Harley name, or any name associated with Harley-Davidson, and even the symbols and logos used in the bikes' graphics. Today, nothing from a pattern oil filter to an item of ladies' underwear can carry a Harley logo without its manufacturer first obtaining an official licence. It is understandable that the factory feels justified in claiming a share of any profits made by individuals using the Harley-Davidson name. They also want to ensure that they and their dealers do not lose out to suppliers of pattern spares.

By 1990, Harley's attitude had come full circle, undoubtedly under the influence of Willie G.

Harley 3 cylinder built by Florida enthusiast - three Shovelheads in a line.

Davidson, and stemming back to the time of the AMF takeover. It was then that Willie G. hung up his white collar and tie forever, and donned the garb of the all-American 'biker', an official, if unilateral acceptance that Harley's cult status and the unsavoury image of the roughneck biker were part of Harley-Davidson's heritage and should be embraced. In a commercial sense, the company came around to realizing the potentially huge market in the

Above: Cycle Fab man, Dave Perewitz, and his own personalized transport.

Left: Dave Perewitz's work on a Harley Streetbike. His skills in engraving and painting have made his company, Cycle Fab, one of the most famous customizing houses.

custom Harley 'look' which had grown and developed unfettered for 30 years. The reviled 'bikers' who first came to public consciousness with the Hollister incident and subsequent publicity, were now seen as the customers. The Harley custom cult had grown bigger than Harley-Davidson itself.

The *Springer Softail* is the absolute proof of this. Other 'new' Harleys, like the *Heritage Softail*, mimic old Harley models, in that case the Hydra Glide Panhead of 1950. The Springer, although using the front suspension system of pre-1950, has no ancestral equivalent. It is a factory 'chopper' and a copy of the style of bike favoured by customizers during the 1960s and 1970s, typified in the *Easy Rider* film.

Today, Harley-Davidson design is drawn from every aspect of Harley's colourful past, sometimes from official sources, sometimes an aspect of a bootleg machine will have caught the designer's eye. Whatever the detail, wherever its fountainhead, it is always unmistakeably *Harley*.

71

A Race to the Finish

To the casual observer, the idea of racing a Harley-Davidson is about as appropriate as water-skiing behind a tug-boat. In truth, however, Harley-Davidson has a racing history longer and more illustrious than any other marque in existence today.

It continues too, with Harleys still showing the competitive edge in American dirt-track racing and in twin-cylinder drag racing. In terms of inter-factory competition successes, Harleys were taking trophies as short a time ago as 1986, in the *Battle of the Twins* series in America. Admittedly, there was a lack of suitable Japanese motors to offer serious competition; still, Gene Church riding the aptly named *Lucifer's Hammer* took the title three years running from 1984 to 1986.

Harley-Davidson's racing history began with the first production bike out of that shed in the Davidson's back garden, way back in 1908. President of Harley-Davidson, Walter Davidson, was the pilot and his mount a *Silent Gray Fellow*. He won the seventh annual Federation of American Motorcyclists' endurance and reliability run. He beat 16 other marques. Thereafter, it was speed

The 1968 factory racer – the KR750. Only a handful remain in the world. This example, complete with official documentation, is valued in 1991 at $750,000.

which would assume a greater importance in the minds of racers and spectators.

It was not until 1913, however, that Harley-Davidson officially supported a race team, leaving it to privateers to carry the flag for them before this. With the newly-appointed Bill Ottaway running the engine development and race department, the so-called *Wrecking Crew* was on its way to racing victory. Rather aptly, the first venue

also known as the *Wigwam,* had been running an eight-valver for a couple of seasons and only just managing to hold off the *Wrecking Crew.* Now, however, there was no stopping them. The bike won the 200-mile International Road Race Championship at Marion, Indiana, where it was ridden by the famous Leslie 'Red' Parkhurst, who was coaxed out of retirement to race with the *Wrecking Crew.*

Harleys featured in competition

smashing debut, winning the 100-mile race and becoming the first rider ever to cover that distance in less than an hour. He was National Champion by the end of the year. He became a full-time *Crew* member in 1930, riding Harleys in board-track events, cross-country endurance races and hill-climbs. He reached the pinnacle of his racing career in 1935 when he won all 13 rounds of the AMA National Championship on dirt-track on a

where the *Wrecking Crew* made their presence felt, was Dodge City, Kansas, in a 300-mile race against arch-rivals Indian, Excelsior, Merkel, Pope and Thor. It was actually won by an eight-valve Indian, but the *Crew* put up a really impressive show. In subsequent races, the Indians were gradually fought off and by 1916, the *Wrecking Crew* was in control, with a hugely successful year.

After the war, Bill Ottaway's newly-developed eight-valve 61 cu inch machine kept up the momentum. The Indian factory,

throughout the 1920s and were scoring victories abroad too, notably in Britain, ridden by names such as Freddie Dixon and F.A. Longman at classic tracks such as Brooklands. It was during this period, back in America, that one of the most famous and influential Harley racers ever came to the fore: Joe Petrali.

Petrali raced for Indian, but was snapped up by the *Wrecking Crew* when he found himself without a mount at the board track at Altoona, Pennsylvania, on 4 July, 1925. Petrali made a record-

The official documentation that accompanies the KR750 shown on the previous page.

Harley *Peashooter* single. In 1937 it was Joe Petrali who rode the new-model 61E overhead valve *Knucklehead* to a still unbroken world record speed of 136mph at Daytona Beach.

Harley-Davidson continued its domination of domestic racing for the next 20 years, with the developing 45 sidevalve engine powering the racebikes to victory.

In 1952 Harley introduced the K model 45 engine to replace the 883 cc (55 cu inch) racer version which came in 1954 was named the KR, and after early teething troubles (i.e., it was not as fast as the machine it replaced), established itself as a classic racing motor. In 1955, the KRs won a 1-2-3 at Daytona, fronted by 19-year old Brad Andres. The KR would win Daytona in 1956, 1957, 1958 and 1959.

the acquisitive Castiglioni brothers who were building their Cagiva empire. During the 17-year association, though, the Italian factory built some completely astounding racing bikes with noteworthy successes.

They began by race-tuning their *A la Verde* model, later re-designated the *Wisconsin*, then rather more commercially appropriate, the *Sprint* for the American market. This was a single

– Harleys are big four-stroke twins after all, not blue smoke-belching screaming strokers. The bikes were built and developed in Italy and had little or no technical input from Milwaukee. To compete with – and beat – the technically advanced Japanese factory entries was a remarkable feat indeed, and Harley-Davidson must have benefited collaterally by having their name associated with such a highly successful bike.

A KR750 dirt-tracker of the early 1950s, stripped bare for action. The sidevalve engine bike would be superseded by the OHV XR750.

VIVA ITALIA!

In 1960, Harley-Davidson took over the Italian Aermacchi factory. Italians have an inate propensity to race anything with two wheels and the fresh capital injected into their ailing company had the race department jumping in enthusiasm. The association would last until 1977, when the interest in the Italian factory was sold on to

cylinder four-stroke 250 laid flat, and was bored to 350 cc. Italian star, Renzo Pasolini took the 350 to a third position in the 350 World Championship in 1966. In 1969, Kel Carruthers raced the bike at the Isle of Man TT in Great Britain impressing all, and seriously worrying the superfast Yamaha two stroke 350s.

Aermacchi Harley-Davidson's real results came in the 1970s after developing a two-stroke aircooled twin. Harley would never crow about the World Championship success Walter Villa brought them

The Italian team with Villa piloting, took three successive 250 cc (15 cu inch) world championships on the twin, in 1974, 1975 and 1976 and the 350 cc (21 cu inch) championship the year after, with a larger capacity version. It was in the same year that Harley-Davidson severed the short but successful Italian connection. Nevertheless, the bikes are still on display at the Rodney C. Gott Museum at the York, Pennsylvania, factory, an interesting, if somewhat incongruous, facet of Harley history.

POWER UP!
Thundering four-stroke Harley racing, as tradition demands, was provided with the advent of the XR750. The bike this replaced was of ageing design, a sidevalve machine designated the KR750. The AMA graciously bent and adjusted their rules to give the KR an advantage over the British onslaught of lightweight, fast and fine-handling bikes during the 1950s and 1960s. When the XR750 was unleashed on to the short circuits and dirt-tracks of the United States, the bike was bold enough to stand up for itself.

Cal Rayborn and Jay Springsteen shot the XRs to fame and classic status. The bikes came in roadrace trim with fairing and clip-ons, or in naked dirt-tracker glory, the latter shunning such 'fancy' notions as a front brake. The bike was basically a sleeved-down 883 Sportster featuring overhead valves. They produced a healthy 62bhp. Handling was

reported by the above racers and test pilots, to be superior to the KR.

Around the asphalt racetracks, the Japanese were coming into their own at this time and the XR750, fast as it was, could barely keep up. Dirt-tracking was the XR's forte, its big 'torquey' motor being perfectly suited to the mile ovals. Springsteen took the 1976, 1977 and 1978 AMA dirt-track championship with consummate ease.

On the short circuits, the bike was really outclassed by fearsome Japanese two-strokes and four-cylinder DOHC motors, except in the twins series – the *Battle of the Twins*. Jerry Branch, noted Harley tuner, developed the XR750 engine, and his work resulted in the building of the XR1000. The motor has also been mated with the

XR750 dirt-racer in the Harley Show at Daytona Speedway. Three times AMA champion, Jay Springsteen rode this bike successfully in the mile and half mile flat tracks.

chassis of Erik Buell, another ex-Harley man, who builds his own hot roadrace chassis for Harley unit motors. Tuned versions of the motor produced around 112bhp, and with Gene Church at the helm, won the championship three years running from 1984 to 1986. He rode a Buell in 1987.

Today, the Ducati 851 has taken the twins into a new hi-tech high-power realm Harley owners can only dream of. However, there is official factory confirmation of a project underway to develop a liquid cooled five-valve per cylinder, fuel injected, short-stroke 45 degree twin to put Harley-Davidson back in the frame. What series the bike would contest though, is not clear; the *Battle of the Twins*, of course, but there is no world series for factory produced one-off racers, apart from the FIM 500 cc World Championship, where the bike would be hopelessly outclassed by two-strokes.

Meanwhile, Harley-Davidson

fans can witness some of the closest and most exciting racing ever to be seen in the AMA Sport Twins class, which has been created just for the 883 Sportster, with Harley-Davidson as the official sponsor. The rules allow very little modification, keeping the cost to entrants down and the competitive edge razor-sharp. The series has

become so popular in the United States, that the support race for the Daytona 200 is actually the Sport Twins final.

Harleys may be the slowest, most ponderous cruisers around, but as long as the factory is in business, there will always be somebody out there, pulling on his leathers, ready to race the classic twin.

Harley-Davidson 250 cc with the successful rider Jay Springsteen at Daytona Speedway, 1978. In 1974, 1975 and 1976, this Italian Aermacchi Harley-Davidson ridden by Walter Villa won the world 250 cc Championship. In 1976, the 350 cc World Championship was also won on this 2-stroke Harley, which beat strong Japanese opposition.

INDEX

Illustrations are denoted by page numbers in italic

FLH Duo-Glide of 1959 in its original colours of Calypso Red with Birch White tank panels.